Classic
Backcountry
Skiing

Also Available from the Appalachian Mountain Club

AMC White Mountain Guide
24th Edition

AMC Maine Mountain Guide
6th Edition

AMC Massachusetts and Rhode Island Trail Guide
6th Edition

Southern Snow:
The Winter Guide to Dixie
by Randy Johnson

Wilderness Search and Rescue
by Tim J. Setnicka

North Woods: An Inside Look at the
Nature of the Northeast
by Peter J. Marchand

At Timberline: A Nature Guide to the
Mountains of the Northeast
by Frederic L. Steele

Forest and Crag: A History of Hiking, Trail
Blazing, and Adventure in the Northeast Mountains
by Laura and Guy Waterman

Classic Backcountry Skiing

A Guide to the Best Ski Tours in New England

David Goodman

APPALACHIAN MOUNTAIN CLUB

BOSTON

Cover photograph: Winter sunset on Mt. Lincoln, Franconia Ridge, New Hampshire. Inset photograph: Sue Minter skiing on Boott Spur, Presidential Range, New Hampshire. Photos by Peter Cole.

All photographs are by the author unless otherwise credited.

Excerpts from David O. Hooke, *Reaching That Peak: 75 Years of the Dartmouth Outing Club* (Canaan, N.H.: Phoenix Publishing, 1987), reprinted with permission.

Published by the Appalachian Mountain Club
Distributed by The Talman Company

Library of Congress Catalog-in-Publication Data

Goodman, David, 1959–
    Classic backcountry skiing : a guide to the best ski tours in New
  England / by David Goodman.
      p. cm.
    Bibliography: p.
    ISBN 0-910146-74-8
    1. Cross-country skiing—New England—Guide-books. 2. New England—Description and travel—1981– —Guide-books. I. Title. II. Title: Classic backcountry skiing.
GV854.5.N35G66 1988
796.93'0974—dc19   88-24260

**Due to changes in conditions, use of the
information in this book
is at the sole risk of the user.**

Printed in the United States of America

10 9 8 7 6 5 4 3 2 1   89 90 91 92 93

*To my parents,
George and Dorothy Goodman*

A Note to Readers

Over time, trails may be rerouted or access altered. The author welcomes comments, corrections, and suggestions so that changes can be made in future editions. Send all correspondence to: Editor, AMC Books, 5 Joy St., Boston, MA 02108.

Contents

Preface

Welcome to the world of backcountry skiing.

It is a world familiar to many of you. It is the hiking trails you climb on, the mountain summits you stop to admire, the trails you wonder about when you look on a map. It includes trailless peaks and well-trodden mountain paths.

To others, this is a new place. You may have been skiing at touring centers at the base of the big peaks. Or you have been downhill skiing on the "front side" of many of these mountains, possibly curious about the world that lies on the side of the ridge without chairlifts. This book is about that world.

"Is it cross-country or downhill skiing?" ask skiers of today. The answer is that it is both. Backcountry skiing is the full spectrum of what you do with skis on your feet: going uphill, downhill, across mountain summits, along river valleys. It is skiing off of groomed trails and prepared snow. This style of skiing goes by many names. Some call it ski mountaineering. Others call it *off-piste* (off-trail) skiing, ski touring, mountain skiing, telemarking, Nordic skiing, or cross-country skiing. In some ways it encompasses all of the above, but in other ways it resists categorization. The most accurate terminology is what it was called fifty years ago: just *skiing*.

Equipment for backcountry skiing is distinctly Nordic, with free heels and light skis. Nordic ski equipment is unmatched as an efficient and enjoyable means of travel to reach the best untouched snow in remote places. But the skiing techniques, which include bringing telemark and parallel turns back into the Nordic skier's repertoire, are a hybrid of cross-country and downhill. Much backcountry skiing is in the mountains, which naturally means that skiing downhill is a major part of the experience. "Down-mountain skiing" was the term skiers from the 1930s used to describe this style of downhill skiing in the backcountry.

Backcountry skiing is full of surprises. It enables you to travel to quiet places, where the snow is untracked, perhaps changing texture with each mile. It also takes you to exciting places, such as high summits with breathtaking snowfields and expansive views all around.

Backcountry skiing is a journey, not necessarily with a destination, in which you are open to whatever comes along. Sometimes the goals of the journeys are introspective. Other times, they are light-hearted, the only goal being to travel under one's own power through the winter wilderness. In either case, the backcountry journey requires an exploratory mind-set, a spirit of adventure and an acceptance that nothing will turn out quite as you planned. Just as the character of a trail changes with each storm, even when the topography remains constant, the experience you have each time you fasten on skis and head into the mountains is never the same as it was before.

This is a book about backcountry skiing in the mountains of New England. Since the 1940s, people have been using cross-country skis on the fields and old logging roads of New England, and downhill skiers have been riding chairlifts to get to their ski trails. Most of these skiers have considered wilderness areas and undeveloped mountains inaccessible. Throughout the 1930s, however, backcountry skiing in the mountains was a passion pursued by many people in New England. The search for the perfect ski run down a mountain was underway in every corner of the Northeast. The highest peaks of the north country—Mount Mansfield, Mount Washington, Mount Cardigan, Mount Greylock—all became home to famous ski trails. These trails, with names like the Thunderbolt, Nose Dive, Teardrop, and Snapper, still bring a surge of adrenaline and satisfaction to skiers today.

My intent with this book is to encourage Nordic skiers to return once again to the high and wild places of New England. I have tried to recapture the spirit of adventure that led the skiers of an earlier generation to head to the mountains and explore. The ski tours in this book are only a sampling.

There are numerous other peaks, open woods, slides, and drainages that offer first-rate skiing to those willing to explore them. The world of the backcountry skier is, after all, every place in the wilderness where it is white.

Acknowledgments

This book represents a community effort. Whether for providing company on the trail, a floor on which to lay my sleeping bag, or invaluable insights about their favorite areas, I am indebted to many people. Long nights of driving across Route 2 in northern New England were made brighter by the thought of friends on the other end who would be welcoming me and joining me on the next leg of the journey.

My sincere thanks go to the following people for their advice, suggestions, hospitality, or other help: Archie Brodsky, Craig Burt, Jr., Dan Gluck, Dick Hall, Jack Handy, Sel Hannah, Ben Kligler, Brian Kunz, Eve LaPlante, Sheryl Lechner, Charlie Lord, Frank Lowenstein, Georges Melas-Kyriazi, Bobby Minter, Sue Morrello, and Rick Strimbeck.

I am particularly indebted to my fearless crew of fellow instructors and friends at the Hurricane Island Outward Bound School, who alternately followed me and dragged me down numerous trails in their enthusiastic support for this effort. They were the one group of people I could count on to show up at a remote trailhead, skis in hand, almost anywhere in New Hampshire or Maine with only one or two hours' notice. Among them are Michael Bowe, Howard and Gail Cohen, Jack Flanagan, Jonathan Goldberg, Jeff Kuller, Paul Nicolazzo, Kevin ("K2") Moore, Anne Morse, Lee Spiller, Elaine Suddeth, and Dave Walker.

Thanks also go to the following companies, which generously provided me with equipment during my research: Karhu USA, Gregory Mountain Products, Kenko International, Feathered Friends, and Rossignol Ski Company.

Special thanks go to Steve Barnett, Peter Cole, Todd Eastman, and Bill Minter for their help. Susan Cummings, my editor at AMC Books, has given wise and patient guidance to this project from its beginnings. This book has also benefitted from the talents of Gail Simon and Sue Seger, production coordinator and marketing coordinator, respectively, at AMC Books. Special thanks also go to Sue Minter, with whom I have shared much in these mountains.

I am grateful to my parents, George and Dorothy Goodman, who have been a source of support, advice, and friendship through all stages of this book, as have Steven, Amy, and Dan Goodman.

Part I

THE WORLD OF BACKCOUNTRY SKIING

The New England Renaissance

Backcountry skiing is not a new sport in New England. It is actually a revival of a sport that enjoyed its heyday in the 1930s and has been in a period of dormancy until recently.

The first skiers in New England were Scandinavian loggers and railroad builders in the mid-1800s. They formed the first ski club in the United States in Berlin, New Hampshire, in 1882. It was later named the Fridtjof Nansen Ski Club, after the famous Norwegian Arctic explorer who skied across Greenland in 1888. Skis began appearing in Hanover, New Hampshire, and in North Adams, Massachusetts, by the turn of the century, and the popularity of the sport slowly began to pick up.

Mountain skiing began attracting interest soon after people gained some basic proficiency with the unwieldy new mode of transportation. The first ski ascent and descent of Mount Marcy in the Adirondacks was accomplished in 1911; Mount Washington was skied (via the auto road) in 1913; and Mount Mansfield was first skied in 1914 via the toll road. Ski racing began gaining interest at Dartmouth College in Hanover, New Hampshire, around the same time.

Skiers of this early era would immerse themselves in all aspects of the sport. They were typically proficient at ski jumping, downhill, slalom, and cross-country skiing, sometimes called *langlauf,* or long-run, skiing. Since people would use the same skis for everything, there was little difference

Crossing the finish line in a 1938 race on the Thunderbolt Trail, Mount Greylock. Photo courtesy of Bill Linscott.

between cross-country and downhill skiing except in where people chose to ski. In the 1920s, ski bindings consisted of a toe bar with a leather heel strap, much like today's cable bindings. Skis were long, heavy hickory boards without metal edges, and boots were the leather hiking-style variety with a box-shaped toe.

Throughout the 1920s, New England skiers looking for downhill skiing opportunities sought out narrow summer hiking trails, logging roads, and streambeds. This was not the easiest terrain to ski, and skiers soon began searching for more open downhill slopes. Katharine Peckett, the daughter of an affluent inn owner near Franconia, New Hampshire, decided after returning from a vacation in Switzerland to clear a small hill near her father's inn. She opened the first ski school in the United States in 1929. It was around this same time that skiers began to make forays into Tuckerman Ravine. The first official downhill race in the country was held on Mount Moosilauke in 1927. While ski touring through the woods was still an enjoyable pastime, skiers were increasingly drawn to the thrill of a good downhill run, and they would travel long and far to find the mountains with the best downhill skiing.

By the 1930s, skiing had captured the imagination of New Englanders. In 1931, the first "snow trains" for skiers left North Station in Boston headed for New Hampshire, and snow trains to Vermont began rolling out of New York City. Within its first year of operation, the Boston & Maine snow train transported 8,371 passengers to New Hampshire; that figure jumped to more than 10,000 the following year. Equipment evolved to keep pace with the rise in interest in downhill skiing. Skis with metal edges appeared, and metal cable bindings, which offered the option of latching down the heel cable for skiing downhill on steeper terrain, were introduced.

A major catalyst for ski activity in the region came about as a direct result of the Depression. The Civilian Conservation Corps (CCC) was created by President Franklin Roosevelt in March 1933 to provide work for unemployed men. It had the dual purpose of addressing national conservation needs and providing jobs. In its nine years of existence, the CCC mobilized 3 million men, who worked throughout the United States on reforestation, trail construction, land erosion, fire control, and construction of dams, bridges, and buildings.

The CCC will be remembered best by New England skiers for the numerous ski trails that it built. Vermont was the greatest beneficiary in this regard, since the state's CCC contingent was under the supervision of Perry Merrill, an avid skier. Under Merrill's direction the CCC cut some of the most famous ski runs in the East, many of which endure and are included in this book, including the Nose Dive, Teardrop, Bruce, Ski Meister, Perry Merrill, and (Charlie) Lord trails on Mount Mansfield. In New Hampshire, their contributions include the Richard Taft Trail on Cannon Mountain, the Alexandria Trail on Mount Cardigan, the Gulf of Slides Trail near Mount Washington, and the Wildcat Trail on the north side of Wildcat Mountain. Many of their other contributions to skiing in New England are cited elsewhere in this book.

Charlie Lord, the master designer of the CCC trails on Mount Mansfield, explained in a personal interview what his formula was for creating the high-quality runs for which the CCC became famous: "The only guide we had was we tried to make them interesting for ourselves—we were a selfish bunch, you know. The trails were made for a fairly good skier—not experts, but we tried to pick a route that would challenge us." Very few of the CCC men were actually skiers, since skiing was even then a sport of the middle and upper classes. "But," says Lord, "some of them were quite enthused about skiing" and enjoyed coming out to watch the big ski races that took place on their trails.

The construction of the CCC ski trails initiated a new era of "down-mountain skiing." This was the term used to describe downhill skiing in the backcountry. Down-mountain trails, also called "walk-up" trails because skiers had to hike up them in order to ski down them, defined the character of skiing in the early 1930s. On some of the longer trails, such as the Bruce Trail on Mount Mansfield, hiking up and skiing down just once took a full day. These outings often proved to be mountaineering adventures as much as they were skiing adventures.

A few select trails were challenging enough to merit classification as Class A race trails. This meant they had approximately 2,000 feet of vertical drop within a specified distance (none of the trail designers seem to recall the exact specifications). The Class A trails of New England included the Nose Dive, the Richard Taft Trail, the Wildcat Trail, the Thunderbolt Trail, and the Pine Hill Trail on Wachusett Mountain. These were the only trails where a racer could receive a coveted rating based on his or her time. "A" racers were the fastest, while "B" and "C" racers were close behind.

Ski technique was evolving from telemark and snowplow to styles more suited to racing. Christiana and stem turns, which marked the beginnings of parallel skiing technique, were being advocated by the better coaches, and people quickly abandoned the graceful old telemark in favor of the faster parallel turn.

The popularity of the CCC trails also signaled a subtle change in the direction that skiing was taking. Exploration of the mountains on skis was taking a back seat to skiing on the established down-mountain trails. These wide ski trails were simply a joy to ski. They were a welcome relief from the difficult hiking trails.

Abner Coleman confessed in the Appalachian Mountain Club journal, *Appalachia,* in 1936:

> The direction of the movement in Vermont is following the widespread preference for downhill running. To some extent this delightful obsession is unfortunate, if only because it leaves a lot of ideal terrain to the mercy of snowshoers. . . . The winter countryside is but little used even by those who live in it. The stampede, rather, both of natives and visitors, has been toward the localities providing down-mountain runs.

The heyday of the down-mountain trails was relatively brief. In 1934, the first rope tow was introduced at a ski hill in Woodstock, Vermont. Within seven years, J-bars, T-bars, and chairlifts sprang up on almost every major ski mountain in New England. There was even an aerial tramway built on Cannon Mountain in New Hampshire. The CCC trails often became the nucleus of the new downhill ski areas, as was the case with the Nose Dive on Mount Mansfield at Stowe, the Wildcat Trail in the Wildcat Ski Area, and the Richard Taft Trail in the Cannon Mountain Ski Area. Those trails that were not crowned with a chairlift were often abandoned, to be reclaimed by weeds and shrubs. This was the fate of a number of trails, including the now defunct Chin Clip and Steeple Trail on Mount Mansfield and the Katzensteig Trail on Wildcat Mountain.

But many of the down-mountain trails survived. Some, like the Snapper Trail on Mount Moosilauke, were preserved as hiking trails, while others, such as the Teardrop and Bruce Trails on Mount Mansfield and the Tucker Brook Trail on Cannon, were maintained by dedicated down-mountain skiers. These people often cleared the trails in defiance of new state and federal regulations that forbade skiing on trails not considered "safe" for the new breed of lift-served skiers. The renegade old-timers, typically alpine skiers during the 1950s and 1960s, were determined to preserve the experience of down-mountain skiing. They were not prepared to part with skiing in powder and interesting snow conditions on mountain trails, where they could escape the icy mogul fields of the crowded lift-served trails.

Frazier Noble, one of the down-mountain skiing holdouts who periodically goes with friends to maintain the Pine Hill Trail on Wachusett Mountain, explained in a personal interview:

> It's hard to convey to people who haven't done any walking for skiing what the experience is about. It's quite different than just buying an impersonal lift ticket and skiing the mountain from the top. You work hard for the run and get far more exercise than you do when just downhill skiing. The scenery is also an important part of it. These trails were not just a slash down a mountain, they had a lot of interesting natural rolls and turns in them. Also, when you walk up you have time to have long chats with people you're skiing with— that's part of the whole ski experience, too.

The advent of lift-served skiing was the knell of death—or at least suspended animation—for backcountry skiing. Those who once flocked to the mountains of the north country to explore new ski routes were now bombing down the downhill slopes of Vermont and New Hampshire. Skiers of the era recall how the number of people skiing in the backcountry around places like Mount Mansfield dropped from about forty on a typical weekend in the early 1930s to no more than a half dozen by the mid-forties.

The evolution in ski equipment epitomized what was happening to the sport of skiing. Rigid downhill boots and fixed bindings that locked down the heel made skiing uphill or even on flat terrain unfeasible. The new gear was strictly for skiing downhill. By the 1950s, the sport of cross-country skiing evolved its own specialized equipment, consisting of lightweight, skinny racing equipment designed for use on prepared, generally flat, ski trails. The split between "downhill" and "cross-country" skiing was institutionalized by the equipment. This division was exaggerated and perpetuated until the late 1970s.

People who were cross-country skiing in the mountains in the 1950s and 1960s were a relatively small and hardy bunch. Joe Pete Wilson, a member of the 1960 Olympic biathlon team who skied in the Green Mountains and the Adirondacks, remembers that it was in the mid-1960s, when he was working at a ski resort, that people heard about him and came to ask him about cross-country skiing. He gave a few lessons and answered people's questions. Their interest was piqued when they saw high school and college students who were out cross-country skiing. There were also many older people who had done cross-country skiing as kids, or who had parents who skied cross-country. They didn't know what kind of skiing they and their parents did, they just knew it was skiing.

The revival of cross-country skiing was also starting to take place at colleges such as Dartmouth. Dartmouth's downhill ski team and its coach, Al Merrill, were nationally renowned. But students noticed that Merrill and a few of his friends "would go out 'touring' after hours," it is reported in David Hooke's *Reaching That Peak*, a history of the Dartmouth Outing Club (DOC). In 1964, Merrill "was persuaded to give the

DOC 'several pointers on ski touring.' By January 1965 ski touring 'was fast becoming the winter's most popular sport.'" In March 1965, a DOC newsletter stated:

> [DOC] managed a surprising number of ski touring trips this winter despite the often filthy snow conditions. Large numbers of men, most of whom traveled on hand-hewn skis garnished with make-shift bindings, glided through weather as diverse as red klister and blue stick. It's a good feeling when your ski sticks on the kick and slides on the glide—an occasional bright eye, raised brow and incredulous mouth numbly muttering "Christ, it works!!!"

A turning point in the popularity of cross-country skiing was the sudden availability of inexpensive skis. In the mid-1960s, the first fiberglass downhill skis came on the market. People quickly traded in their old wooden models, which were easily converted into cross-country skis with a little shaving and narrowing to lighten them up. Hooke reports that at Dartmouth, "it is understandable, given the spirit of the times, why touring would have had such appeal: not only was there now a whole lot of obsolete downhill equipment, but converting it and using it would be a great way to get away from 'it all'—meaning lift lines, crowds, and the other trappings of the 'new' Alpine skiing of the day."

In 1970 Joe Pete Wilson and William Lederer co-authored *The Complete Cross Country Skiing and Ski Touring.* According to what the authors have been told, it quickly became one of the best-selling instructional books ever written. It was a sign that change was in the air.

The 1970s saw the growth of cross-country skiing at ski touring centers. But by the late 1970s another small-scale revival began brewing within the world of cross-country skiing. A small group of mountaineers-turned-skiers, cross-country ski instructors, and alpine skiers who had grown bored with the lift-area scene wanted to add some adventure to their ski experience. They were getting restless, and touring center skiing was simply not enough to entertain them anymore. They wanted to combine their mountain climbing with their skiing, so they began experimenting by trial and error with using downhill skiing techniques on cross-country skis. Cross-country skiers began parallel skiing, and even revived the defunct telemark turn. Experimentation and information sharing were at a high pitch among skiers in the Stowe and Killington areas. The publication of Steve Barnett's now classic *Cross-Country Downhill* in 1978 generated further excitement about the potential for Nordic skiing.

With the renewed interest in backcountry skiing came a concurrent evolution in equipment. The lightweight skis and boots of ski tourers and racers was inadequate for the rigors of backcountry skiing. Karhu and Fischer, both with U.S. headquarters in New England, were two of the first companies to respond to the demand from telemarkers and mountain skiers for a heavy-duty ski. The metal-edged Fischer Europa 77 went on sale in the early 1970s, and the Fischer Europa 99 and Karhu XCD-GT were introduced in 1978 and have been steady sellers ever since. Other manufacturers followed suit, and there is now a wide array of choices available to backcountry skiers.

Skiing has come full circle since the 1930s. Skiers are now in the process of rediscovering the techniques pioneered by an earlier generation. This process of experimentation and the excitement it generates closely resemble the enthusiastic quest of a half-century ago. By reclaiming the downhill component of skiing, Nordic skiers have once again opened up the mountains for exploration on skis. The down-mountain trails have had new life breathed into them—or maybe just had their old spirit restored. It is a spirit of adventure and a love of the mountains, which has an uncanny way of transcending the barriers of time to bring together everyone who feels its pull.

The Ski Tours

The ski tours in this book were chosen because they are "classics." Classic ski tours in New England have a special character. The mountain ranges in this region are unlike any others in the United States. The elevations are small, but the conditions are distinctly alpine.

There are several qualities that are necessary for a tour to be considered a classic.

History. Many of the ski tours were chosen for their historic importance. They were trails that formed the hub of down-mountain skiing activity sixty years ago. Many were built by the Civilian Conservation Corps (CCC) in the 1930s. They represent a slice of New England culture as well as some of the best skiing to be found anywhere. The CCC and other trailblazers in New England had their choice of where the best ski runs would go; the enduring quality and popularity of those trails today are a testament to the keen eye they had for choosing the best routes.

Aesthetics. A classic ski tour must have scenic value that captures the spirit of New England's mountains and forests. What this area lacks in jagged mountain skylines and vast open bowls it makes up for in picturesque birch forests and accessible mountain summits. A classic tour may travel the full range of New England terrain, or it may showcase one aspect of this special landscape.

Quality of Skiing. Classic ski tours include high-quality skiing terrain. Quality here means variety: the best tours hold your interest because they call upon a full range of skiing techniques. A classic tour might include skating on flats, diagonal striding on straightaways, skinning up a mountainside, and telemark and parallel skiing down an exciting powder run. This is total skiing—not a specialized subdivision of the sport.

In short, a classic ski tour has it all.

Difficulty Ratings

The ski tours in this book are intended for experienced cross-country skiers who are comfortable skiing on a variety of terrain. A skier who is proficient on intermediate trails at a ski touring center should be able to ski most of the routes in this book. None of the tours in this book are intended for novice cross-country skiers except those in the section "Easy Day Trips in the White Mountains." These latter trails, though not classics in the sense described here, are nevertheless beautiful and worthwhile tours. I have included them in the hope that they will inspire less-experienced cross-country skiers to continue their development and their explorations as backcountry skiers.

Good downhill skiing opportunities are an important part of every classic ski tour described here. No mountain ski tour is complete without them; indeed, the thrill of a long backcountry downhill run has drawn skiers to the mountains for years. Each tour is rated *moderate, more difficult,* or *most difficult.*

Moderate. The terrain includes gentle hills. A good snowplow technique or step turn should suffice for skiing downhill.

More Difficult. The terrain includes extended, steeper uphill and downhill sections. Proficiency at turning on steeper terrain—using telemark, parallel, snowplow, or other techniques—is necessary.

Most Difficult. The terrain includes sustained downhill skiing on trails that are narrow, very steep, or both. The ability to link quick turns is necessary.

These difficulty ratings are subjective and extremely variable for any given tour. They describe approximately what the trail would be like to ski in average conditions: moderately heavy powder over a solid base that may be broken up by another skier's tracks. But as the saying goes, *conditions are everything*. A tour that is considered "moderate" in powder conditions can be ferocious in breakable crust. An "easy" ski tour can at times challenge the best skiers. You must know your ability to ski in various conditions and know when the conditions of a trail exceed your abilities. There is no shame in deciding to walk down a steep, icy chute that you are not comfortable skiing; in fact, it takes considerable experience to know your limits.

This is a regional rating system. The rating of each tour is relative to the difficulty of other tours in New England. These ratings are not necessarily comparable to guidebook ratings in other areas of the country.

The steepness of some routes is occasionally described in terms of the angle of the slope. Most skiers and climbers tend to overestimate slope angles. The most accurate way to determine the steepness of a slope is with a clinometer, which is built into the top-of-the-line compasses made by Suunto and Silva. Life-Link markets a relatively inexpensive slope meter as well. Becoming proficient in estimating slope angles is especially useful in avalanche hazard assessment, where the difference between a 20-degree slope and 35-degree slope is critical (see the "Mountaineering Skills" section for more on avalanches).

In general, 20-degree slopes are considered advanced intermediate downhill terrain, such as what is encountered on the Sherburne Trail. Slopes of 30 degrees are advanced downhill terrain. They give pause to the vast majority of Nordic skiers, many of whom resort to traversing and kick turning to get down a slope of this grade. The middle and lower section of

Hillman Highway in Tuckerman Ravine fits this description. Forty-degree slopes are the realm of expert skiers. Few Nordic skiers are comfortable on slopes of this severity, particularly if the grade is sustained. An example of the latter is the top of the Tuckerman Ravine headwall, just below the lip.

A Word about Snowmobiles

Occasionally, these ski tours intersect or coincide for a short distance with snowmobile trails. There is often considerable antagonism between skiers and snowmobilers, and I am afraid that skiers must bear an equal share of the blame for whatever bad feelings exist. Skiers do not own the woods. Snowmobilers have as much right to enjoy the outdoors on their designated trails as skiers do on ski routes, however noisy or offensive snowmobiles may be. Furthermore, skiers often depend on the kindness of snowmobilers when an evacuation becomes necessary. I have seen snowmobilers provide help at great inconvenience to themselves when an emergency has arisen.

Skiers should declare peace. A friendly smile or wave to snowmobilers when you are on one of their trails will go far toward restoring some sense of mutual respect and civility to these encounters in the woods. It will also keep you from getting run over.

The New England Ski Season

There is usually good snow cover for skiing in the backcountry of northern New England from mid-December through early April. In many years, skiing has begun by Thanksgiving. Likewise, April snowstorms are not uncommon and are sometimes quite substantial. December and February are the months with the heaviest snowfall in the three northern states, with the snow reaching its greatest depth in late February and early March.

Southern New England enjoys a shorter ski season. Most of the snow falls in January and February. The best time for skiing in central and western Massachusetts is from late December through mid- to late March. The skiing in northern and northwestern Connecticut usually runs from late December to early March, while the best time for skiing in western Rhode Island is January and February.

Spring skiing in New England begins in early April. Mount Washington is the favorite location. Skiing in Tuckerman Ravine often continues through June. (See the Mount Washington Region route descriptions in this book.) There is also spring skiing at higher elevations and in other ravines of the White Mountains, on Mount Mansfield, and on Katahdin.

The New England Winter Environment

Winters in New England are characterized by extremely cold weather. The intensity of the cold is amplified in the mountains, where exposure is greatest and conditions are typically worse than at lower elevations. Data from the weather observatory on Mount Washington illustrates this point. The summit of Mount Washington (elevation 6,288 feet) is under cloud cover about 55 percent of the time. The average winter temperature is 15 degrees Fahrenheit; the record low temperature is -46 degrees. Average winds in the winter are 44 mph, and winds over 100 mph have been recorded every month of the year. These are admittedly some of the most extreme conditions in New England, but it is better to be prepared for the most severe mountain weather than to be caught off guard in the winter.

Table 1 presents a climatological profile of New England in winter.

Table 1
Winter Weather in New England

Location	Mean Snow, Sleet Totals (inches)					Mean Temperature (degrees F)				
	Dec.	Jan.	Feb.	Mar.	Apr.	Dec.	Jan.	Feb.	Mar.	Apr.
Pinkham Notch, N.H.	35.5	31.4	38.2	34.2	16.0	19.9	15.8	17.3	25.6	37.4
Mt. Washington, N.H.	42.5	39.0	40.5	41.8	29.2	9.3	4.8	5.5	12.0	22.5
Woodstock, N.H.	23.6	21.2	24.2	17.4	3.09	23.5	18.8	21.3	30.4	42.3
Montpelier, Vt.	23.8	18.2	23.2	17.4	5.0	20.5	15.1	17.5	27.0	40.4
Mt. Mansfield, Vt.[a]	41.6	36.6	27.8	36.0	24.0	11.1	6.7	11.5	18.0	34.0
Bar Harbor, Me.	14.1	16.1	19.5	12.8	2.6	28.2	23.8	24.6	32.5	42.8
Ripogenus Dam, Me.	28.2	25.7	26.8	20.9	7.4	17.7	11.9	13.3	23.6	36.6
Adams, Mass.	14.2	15.9	17.0	11.9	2.2	26.0	20.7	22.4	31.6	44.3
Fitchburg, Mass.	13.6	16.0	18.3	15.5	3.2	28.7	24.3	25.9	34.4	46.3
Falls Village, Conn.	12.1	13.5	14.0	12.3	3.0	27.8	23.3	26.0	34.2	46.2
Providence, R.I.	5.6	9.6	9.7	5.9	1.0	31.6	28.7	28.6	36.8	46.0

Source: National Oceanic and Atmospheric Administration, *Climatology of the United States, No. 60,* 1951–1973.
[a]Source: Mt. Mansfield weather station, 1982–1987.

Clothing and Equipment

The choice of clothing and equipment you are most comfortable with is a personal one. There is no one right set of clothes or skis that works for every person. There are, however, some basic guidelines that should be taken into consideration when you are looking for new gear.

Dressing to Stay Warm

Clothing for backcountry skiing must keep you warm and relatively dry. Fabrics such as cotton are notorious for being unable to do this. When cotton gets wet, it acts like a towel, keeping saturated fibers next to your skin and drawing out body heat and energy. The best clothes to wear in the winter are those made of wool or of synthetics such as polypropylene and pile, or other equivalent synthetics such as Capilene, Thermax, bunting, Polarfleece, or Synchilla. These fabrics retain very little moisture and dry from the inside out when they get wet. The body heat of an active skier is usually adequate to dry them.

The most effective way to dress to stay warm in winter is to wear a number of lighter layers rather than one bulky layer. This technique is called *layering*. What keeps you warm is air trapped next to your body, not clothing. By wearing a number of loose, lighter layers, you can most efficiently trap air, which is warmed by your body.

For layering to be effective, you must peel a layer *before* you begin sweating profusely. Heavy perspiration in the winter can be dangerous. It can lead to dehydration and will saturate your clothes as if you were standing in the rain.

A typical layering system for an active day of skiing is a polypropylene shirt, a lightweight wool or pile sweater, wool or pile pants, and a windbreaker of nylon or Gore-Tex. In the pack would be a heavy sweater or pile jacket, nylon or Gore-Tex overpants, and a down parka.

Wind protection is especially important in the New England mountains. All the sweaters in your closet won't keep you warm with a 30-mph wind slicing through them. A parka or anorak made of a tight weave and fast-drying fabric such as Gore-Tex is an essential part of any layering system. As your outer layer, this shell should also be water-resistant. Wet snows are common in New England, and don't be surprised if you encounter rain as well.

A common mistake skiers make when dressing is to throw on a down parka and head up the mountain. In my experience, the temperature would have to be well below zero to be comfortable skiing in a down parka. It is simply too much insulation for an aerobic activity like skiing. A good practice is to start skiing while feeling a bit chilled; you will warm up within a few minutes and save having to undress and repack after skiing a few hundred yards.

The Right Tools for the Job

As any builder knows, you can't do a job right without the correct tools. This axiom also applies to skiers. Fifty years ago there was only one type of ski, and it was used for every type of skiing, including ski jumping. Today, ski equipment has become a dizzying forest of specialized gear. There are now different skis for skating, touring on groomed trails, touring off-trail, racing, jumping, lift-area skiing, backcountry tele-marking, and alpine touring.

The best skiers can ski most routes on any equipment. That isn't to say it's the easiest way to go—just that high-tech equipment is no substitute for good technique. Many back-country mountain routes can be done in light touring gear, if that is what you own. But you would probably find most routes a good deal easier to ski, and more enjoyable, with equipment that is better suited to the terrain. Below are some suggestions on what to look for in equipment.

Boots. Good backcountry boots are perhaps the most important investment you will make when upgrading your equipment for backcountry skiing. If you are upgrading piecemeal, it makes sense to buy boots first. A good backcountry ski boot is essentially a hiking boot with a three-pin toe piece. These so-called telemark boots generally have a Norwegian welt construction and a more rigid, high-ankle profile. Their key feature is that they are torsionally rigid. This means that when you twist your leg to turn the ski, the twisting motion is transferred directly into turning power on the ski, instead of into just twisting the boot. You are probably familiar with the terrifying sensation of flying downhill on cross-country skis and seeing the skis flop and chatter all over the place while your boots are flexing uselessly in the bindings. A good, stiff boot will add an element of control to your skiing you may never have experienced before.

You may want to consider buying double boots if you have chronic problems with cold feet. Double boots are heavy but warm. Single boots with insulated supergaiters are another possible solution. (See the section on frostbite for more on this.)

Avoid buying ultrastiff telemark racing boots. The plastic collars and downhill-style buckles on these boots will cause you nothing but pain on uphill climbs and long tours. They are strictly for lift-served skiing.

Unless you can find a pair of used boots, be prepared to pay a relatively hefty price for good boots. They are expensive but an investment that should last many years.

Skis. The ski tours in this book with sections of extended downhill skiing that are rated *more difficult* or *most difficult* are most easily done by the majority of skiers on heavier backcountry or mountaineering-oriented skis—commonly described as telemark skis. Telemark skis are heavy-duty, metal-edged skis that are designed for maximum control on variable, difficult terrain. They tend to be wider than most touring skis, enabling them to float better in powder and to provide a more stable platform for skiers skiing on uneven ground and wearing a heavy pack. Metal edges are particularly useful in the East, where encounters with ice are a fact of life for the backcountry skier.

Metal-edged skis do have a drawback: they are heavy and consequently not as enjoyable to ski with on flatter terrain or long tours. Metal-edged skis are not necessary for skiing in powder or on flat terrain where control on downhills is not a primary consideration.

Ski tours rated as moderate in this book can generally be skied comfortably on touring skis, provided you have sturdy boots and reasonably good snow conditions. A good backcountry touring ski should be fairly wide for flotation in deep snow, have ample sidecut to facilitate turning, and be solidly constructed. One way to assess whether a ski fits these criteria is to place it back-to-back with a general-purpose telemark ski; a good edgeless backcountry ski should have a similar profile and similar measurements. Wood skis have excellent performance characteristics (they are still unmatched for climbing) but are more prone to breaking than are fiberglass models. If you ski with wood skis, be equipped to make a good field repair of a broken ski.

Camber refers to the arch in the middle of the ski; the space created by this arch is called the wax pocket. A double-cambered ski has a stiff arch, while a single-cambered ski has little or no arch. Double-cambered skis are generally considered more appropriate for touring, since they hold wax better over the course of a long tour. Single-cambered skis typically offer more control at high speeds and are preferred by those who ski primarily at lift-served areas. However, many backcountry skiers swear by single-cambered skis when they are used with climbing skins. It is purely a matter of personal preference. Both single- and double-cambered skis are appropriate for mountain skiing.

The debate over which is best, waxless or waxable skis, should really not be so strident here in the East. Waxing skis at cold temperatures is not complicated, and it is made even simpler with the two-wax systems that are available. The tricks of waxing can be learned from other skiers. Waxable skis are faster, quieter, and better climbers than waxless skis. Simply put, a fast ski is a fun ski to tour on.

Where waxless skis come into their own is in snow conditions at temperatures around freezing, when waxing can often be a frustrating hit-or-miss affair. The debate over waxless versus waxable is more relevant in the West, where warm weather skiing is common, than in New England, where we do most of our skiing in colder temperatures. Having waxable skis allows more room for improvising to accommodate the changes in terrain. You can always use red wax to climb with if you don't own skins or ski with just a base wax if you are doing a lot of lift-served skiing.

For a good discussion of how to wax skis, read *Cross-Country Skiing*, by Ned Gillette and John Dostal, or *Cross-Country Ski Gear*, by Michael Brady.

Bindings. Heavy-duty three-pin or cable bindings are the best choice regardless of the type of ski you use. Three-pin bindings designed for telemarking and backcountry skiing are made of strong metal alloys. They are considerably sturdier than standard three-pin bindings. Getting stranded with a mangled lightweight aluminum binding when you are five miles from nowhere should convince you that heavy-duty bindings are worth the extra investment. Check to see that your three-pin bindings come with extra slots for tying on a bail wire or heel attachment, in case the binding breaks or you lose a bail.

Cable bindings are also appropriate for backcountry skiing. They are strong and simple, and are are easily jerry-rigged for repair if they break.

Prototypes have recently been tested for backcountry boot-binding systems similar to those used for touring. As of this writing they are not yet available commercially.

Poles. Most people just use their regular cross-country ski poles for backcountry skiing. A modification may be useful. For downhill skiing on steep trails, long cross-country poles tend to keep you up too high and can throw you off balance. One good solution I've seen is to place a piece of closed-cell foam around the pole about a quarter of the way down from the grip and tape it in place with some duct tape. When skiing downhill, you can then slide your hands down to grasp the poles on this lower grip.

Useful equipment that eliminates the debate over which size poles to take with you on a tour are the adjustable probe poles sold by several manfacturers. These poles can collapse or extend, depending on the demands of the terrain; they can be kept long for the uphill climb and shortened for downhill skiing. They also come with interchangeable baskets and grips that can be alternated depending on the type of skiing you are doing. Finally, they can be joined together to form one 8-foot-long avalanche probe, a useful feature when traveling in avalanche prone terrain.

Climbing Skins. The use of climbing skins on most of these ski tours is strongly recommended. Climbing skins are ski-length strips of fabric with one-directional "hairs." These hairs mat down when skiing forward and grip the snow when the ski starts to slide backward. Today's skins are made out of either nylon, mohair, or plastic. They mimic the action of early skins, which were actually animal pelts that skiers strapped to the bottoms of their skis in order to ski uphill.

When skiing in the mountains, you will often spend at least half a day skiing up steep grades in order to get to a summit or the top of a trail. The ascent on a number of these routes would become so tiring and frustrating without skins that most people would understandably abandon their destination halfway. Skins are actually a safety item in these situations. They permit you to ration your energy efficiently and avoid exhaustion. Also, being able to gain purchase in any type of snow means you can get out quickly with a minimum of effort if the need arises.

Skins can be left on for downhills that you find particularly desperate. They will slow you down considerably, but they also make it difficult to turn.

Skins must be meticulously cared for. They must be dried out after each use and brushed clean when you remove them from your skis. Stick-on skins require a reapplication of glue about once per season.

Nylon and mohair skins are more expensive than plastic ones. The disadvantage of the plastic skins—called "Snake Skins"—is that they have virtually no forward glide and the strap-on arrangement may cause them to roll over the edges of the ski when skiing on a sidehill. However, they are very durable and are good climbers.

Miscellaneous. If you are an avid telemarker and plan to do a lot of backcountry skiing, you should invest in kneepads. Injuries ranging from bruised to broken kneecaps have been increasingly common among telemarkers, but they can usually be prevented by placing a little foam and plastic between you and the ground. Tree stumps, rocks, and ice can all send you flying. The best protection is skateboard kneepads, which have a plastic cup over a layer of closed-cell foam. They are available at skateboarding shops and are also sold by Life-Link. Second best are basketball kneepads, which are just closed-cell foam pads that offer a small amount of additional protection.

Eye protection for skiing through trees or on hiking trails that are not maintained for skiing (such as the Long Trail between Sugarbush and Mad River Glen) is essential. Ski goggles, glacier glasses, or sunglasses with a neck cord will all do the job.

Consider carrying a sleeping bag on more remote day trips. Having a sleeping bag along is a wise safety precaution, particularly if your party is large or includes some inexperienced skiers.

Backcountry Repair

Your equipment *will* break. Backcountry skiing is abusive. Skis snap, bindings rip out, poles turn into pretzels, boot pinholes blow out, and packs detonate at the seams. About the only thing that you can count on is that each of these mishaps will occur at the least convenient moment.

Backcountry skiers should be equipped to perform functional field repairs. Below are basic items needed for a repair kit. This kit can be improved by sharing information with other skiers, many of whom may have a favorite item or repair they've performed. (I would be interested in hearing about other such items or successful "miracle repairs.")

Screwdriver. A #3 Phillips screwdriver fits cross-country binding screws. Chouinard sells a handy Posidrive model, or you can improvise one by filing down the tip of a smaller Phillips screwdriver.

Glue. Quick-drying Superglue works well for everything from securing binding screws to reinforcing a broken ski, but it can leak in your pack. Pack it securely.

Hose Clamps. A small assortment of hose clamps is useful for repairing broken poles and skis. Have some small enough to fit around a pole with aluminum flashing wrapped around it, and large enough to fit around overlapping broken ski ends.

Aluminum Flashing. Aluminum flashing can be used to splint a broken or bent pole or ski. For a pole, wrap a section around the break and hold it in place with hose clamps. Skis can be patched similarly, although it is a more tenuous splint. Curved snow stakes for tents are also useful for splinting poles. Another idea for splinting a ski comes from Allan Bard: use two steel ski scrapers with holes drilled in them to "sandwich" the break. Glue and screw the scrapers on tightly.

Screws. Binding screws love to back themselves out. The best solution is prevention. Put a dab of Shoe-Goo in the screw holes and under the binding before mounting the binding on the ski. Get into the habit of checking your bindings before each outing to make sure the screws are in tightly. Always have on hand a small assortment of screws. Extra binding screws can usually be obtained from a ski shop. A few over-sized screws are useful in case a binding hole becomes stripped.

Steel Wool. Steel wool can be used with glue to fill stripped binding screw holes. It hardens like a steel casing around the screw.

Nylon Cord. Carry at least three meters of it. It is invaluable in binding repair. It can be used to replace a lost bail, or rigged like a cable binding.

Knife. Swiss army knives are useful for spreading peanut butter and for doing just about anything else you can imagine.

Extra Binding. It sure saves a lot of hassle at ten below not have to fiddle with jerry-rigging something that may not work anyway. Ski repair shops often have an extra binding kicking around that they are willing to spare. Note that telemark bindings have a wider spacing between the front and rear screw holes than do lightweight touring bindings. Use the awl on your Swiss army knife to start a new screw hole if you have to.

Duct Tape. When everything else fails . . . so will the duct tape. But have it along anyway. A good way to carry it is to wrap a wad around your poles. And keep a roll in your car to replenish your supply, since it always seems to get used for something.

Mountaineering Skills

Backcountry skiing is really just winter mountaineering on skis—hence the term *ski mountaineering*, which aptly describes most of the ski tours in this book. To travel safely in the winter wilderness, skiers need good mountaineering skills. "Good ski technique," as Steve Barnett writes in *The Best Ski Touring in America*, "rates well behind avalanche knowledge, navigational skills, and camping skills as something you need to know to ski." Some of these skills can be learned from books or classes; others, like good judgment, must be honed by experience.

This book will not attempt to teach mountaineering in any depth. Other books cover the subject thoroughly, and there is little point in repeating what has already been said. A widely respected reference guide that I recommend to people who are new to backcountry skiing is *Mountaineering: The Freedom of the Hills*. However, I will briefly describe the skills in which every backcountry skier should be proficient.

Mountaineering Judgment

Most judgment calls in the mountains ultimately come down to a decision made by one or more people on what margin of safety they are comfortable with. In the winter, travelers need a larger margin of safety than in the summer. An unplanned night out in the snow without adequate equipment can have serious consequences.

Good judgment in the mountains requires taking into consideration a wide range of variables when making decisions. Among other things, you must consider the strength of each individual in your party (Are they strong skiers? Are they in good physical condition?), the condition of each person at the point a decision is being made (Is everybody warm? Is anybody nearing the point of exhaustion?), the objective hazards your party will encounter (How exposed is the route to the elements? Is there significant avalanche danger? What is the weather forecast? What are the snow conditions?), and what you are equipped to accomplish as a group—materially and physically.

Anticipation is the name of the game in the mountains. The more you are prepared for the unlikely, the greater your margin of safety. If you choose to play things close to your limit, you should be prepared for the consequences of the inevitable time when things don't go the way you had planned.

Navigation

Trails can be especially difficult to follow in winter. Blazes on summer hiking trails are often obscured by snow, or are difficult to see, particularly during snowstorms. Whiteouts, which can occur during a heavy snowstorm and be particularly intense on exposed mountain summits, are not uncommon. It is essential therefore that skiers be proficient with a map and compass, and carry both of them in the backcountry. An altimeter, though helpful for pinpointing your location and predicting changes in weather, is not commonly carried by mountaineers in the East, nor is it considered necessary.

Maps are the most important items for navigation. Ideally, if you are closely following a map, the compass should rarely have to come out. The two most common types of trail maps are sketch maps and topographic maps. Sketch maps show the rough outline of trails in an area. They are often not drawn to an accurate scale, may not indicate direction, and do not show changes in elevation. They are useful in combination with topographic maps in determining the approximate location of trails.

A topographic map provides detailed information about the landscape. It is the basic tool of the backcountry traveler. Learning to read topographic maps takes time, but developing a fundamental grasp of how they work is not difficult. Simply put, each contour line represents a gain in elevation. The most common contour intervals used on maps published by the U.S. Geological Survey (USGS) are 10, 20, 40, and 100 feet. Some New England maps have been issued with metric contour intervals. This information is printed at the bottom of each USGS map.

Topographic maps are extremely helpful when planning a ski route because you can tailor the tour to the type of terrain you are seeking. Areas with contour lines bunched tightly together indicate steep slopes, while wider spaces between the lines indicate a more moderate grade. You will get a feel for what type of topography to look for on maps by checking a map when you are skiing and seeing how the terrain is depicted.

The best way to stay oriented with a map is to check it frequently, particularly when you arrive at obvious landmarks. This means keeping the map accessible at all times. If you have to dig in your pack to get it, chances are you won't bother until it is too late. Use the map to predict what is around the next bend and what you will encounter in the next half mile. If the terrain is not what you predicted it would be, you have either miscalculated the distance or are in the wrong place. Either way, you have been alerted to the problem sooner rather than later and can make a quick adjustment.

Maps come in different scales. Maps with a scale of 1:62,500 in the 15-minute series cover an area of about 12 by 18 miles, with nearly 1 inch equal to 1 mile. Maps with a scale of 1:24,000 in the 7.5-minute series cover an area of about 6 by 9 miles, with about 2½ inches equal to a mile. The latter maps are the easiest to navigate from, since they show a smaller area in greater detail than do the 15-minute maps. The USGS is in the process of issuing new maps of New England all in the 7.5-minute scale, replacing the ancient 15-minute maps that have until recently been the standard. Most

USGS maps of Vermont, Massachusetts, Connecticut, Rhode Island, and Maine have been reissued since the late 1960s, but much of the mountain region of New Hampshire is still only covered by the older 15-minute maps. New Hampshire skiers are not stranded, since the Appalachian Mountain Club (AMC) has a variety of maps that cover all of the White Mountains and Mounts Cardigan and Monadnock, mostly in the 1:62,500 scale.

All this having been said, map reading in the Northeast can be a frustrating affair. Mountaineers accustomed to navigating in big western ranges can easily become confused by the small scale of New England terrain. Distant landmarks are often impossible to sight from the forested trails, and small drainages on the map can be indistinct. The keys here are paying attention to small changes in the terrain and looking up to see how you are oriented to whatever distant location you can see. Navigating here is like skiing here: our compact landscape makes everything a little more difficult.

A compass is a hand-held plastic device with a floating magnetic needle inside that points north—almost. The needle actually points to magnetic north, and the angle of deviation from true north must be corrected depending on where you are on the planet. In New England, magnetic declination ranges from 14 degrees west in western Massachusetts and Vermont to 20 degrees west in northern Maine. The exact declination for a given area will be printed on your topographic map. This means that if you take a bearing from a map, you should *add* the amount of declination for that area in order to arrive at an accurate bearing to follow. If you tend to forget whether to add or subtract in the Northeast, think *Add*-irondacks. If you take a bearing from a distant landmark like a mountain summit, you must *subtract* the declination before using the compass bearing on a map. This compensates for the amount that the needle is exaggerating the angle between the distant object and yourself because of its affinity for magnetic north.

Compasses can be used to establish whether or not you are going in the right direction, to pinpoint your position (by triangulation), or to follow a bearing. The latter is particularly useful in dense eastern forests, where following a bearing is sometimes the only way to bushwhack your way out of the deep woods if you've gotten totally spun around. Remember that compasses are not the only indicators of direction of travel. You can always use the sun—which rises in the east, spends most of the day in the south, and sets in the west. When you've really gotten waylaid, remember that the moon also rises in the east, and the north star points north.

Winter Camping

Knowing how to comfortably spend a night outdoors in the winter opens up exciting new possibilities for backcountry skiers. Multiday ski tours can be planned and remote wilderness explored. It is also important for skiers to know how to spend a night safely in winter in the event they are benighted through unforeseen circumstances.

Many of the principles of dressing to stay warm apply to sleeping warm. The key is to preserve and generate as much body heat as possible. This may be done in several ways.

The basic equipment for preserving body heat while sleeping is a sleeping bag and an insulating ground pad. A sleeping bag keeps you warm by trapping air next to your skin. The more *loft*, or trapped air, a sleeping bag has, the warmer it is. A winter sleeping bag should have at least six inches of loft, which will keep most people warm in temperatures to about 0 degrees Fahrenheit. Both down and synthetic (such as Polarguard and Quallofil) sleeping bags are appropriate, although down bag users must take care to keep their bags dry. If you do not own a winter sleeping bag, two lighter bags, with one inside the other, should be sufficient.

A good sleeping bag is useless in the snow without insulation beneath it. Sleeping pads made of Ensolite, Evasote, or other closed-cell foams do a good job of insulating you from the snow, but often one pad is not enough. The more space between you and the ground, the warmer you will be. In addition to using your sleeping pad, consider sleeping on extra clothes, on an extra sleeping pad, or on your pack. Also, be sure that your sleeping pad is rated to withstand temperatures below zero. Summer pads, although they may look the same, will crack at low temperatures.

Winter mountaineers should know how to construct an emergency snow shelter. Snow has remarkable insulating properties. That is one of the reasons hibernating animals can stay alive when they dig themselves into the snow for the winter. If you get benighted without adequate equipment, digging a snow cave may save your life. The temperature inside a snow cave can easily be 30 degrees warmer than the outside air. There are many types of snow shelters that work. See the bibliography for books that cover the subject, and spend a day playing with a shovel in your backyard to try your hand at building several different types of shelters.

Even with a good sleeping bag, your body will have to have enough caloric fuel to generate heat throughout the night. The best fuel is high-carbohydrate foods such as pasta, which should be eaten in quantity before going to bed. In addition, keep a bag of quick-acting, high-energy food such as gorp next to you as you sleep. If you get cold during the night, eating a few handfuls of gorp may be all you need to keep your furnace burning.

Avalanche Awareness

Avalanches pose a serious danger to skiers. The fact that New England does not have *a lot* of avalanches should not be confused with the notion that we do not have *any*. New England has less of the type of terrain and snow conditions that favor avalanches, but it does have its share. And an avalanche in New England is as deadly as an avalanche in Colorado.

The danger of avalanches is greatest on slopes of 30–45 degrees. This danger is at its peak in the first twenty-four hours after a large snowstorm. The ski routes described in this book that are most prone to avalanche are Tuckerman Ravine, Katahdin, and the Gulf of Slides. In addition, any ravines, gullies, slides, or steep open slopes that you might be skiing can avalanche when the necessary combination of conditions exists.

Most ski tours in New England are relatively safe from the threat of avalanches. We have few steep open slopes above timberline where snow instability becomes a major concern.

The more you develop an interest in backcountry skiing, the more you need to know about avalanches. This is especially true if you plan to venture to mountains in the western United States and elsewhere. Read books, take courses, and ask questions of people with experience in avalanche hazard assessment. The Appalachian Mountain Club offers a good introductory avalanche course in Pinkham Notch every winter. (See the bibliography for recommended books on the topic.)

Self-reliance

Being self-reliant in the mountains has long been a basic ethic of mountaineers. Having the ability to be self-reliant requires proficiency in first aid and mountaineering skills. But just as important as these skills is a mind-set when heading into the mountains that your party will not count on being bailed out by someone else if an accident occurs. Traveling with this mind-set should factor into your choice of route, equipment, and skiing companions.

Self-reliance is important on a practical level. Rescues take a long time, particularly in winter. If an injury is life threatening, time may be of the essence.

A problem has developed in recent years as people have come to assume that a rescue is just around the corner whenever they head to the hills. Many people have become lazy or careless about preventive safety measures. Being in the mountains without extra clothing, first aid provisions, and repair equipment is inviting trouble. The odds favoring mishaps always seem to increase in direct proportion to poor preparation.

First Aid

Prevention is the key to avoiding winter emergencies. Recognizing symptoms and being alert to the condition of members of your party are critical. Medical emergencies in winter are a different ballgame than in the summer. The extreme environment increases stress on both the victim and rescuer, and problems can progress from slight to life threatening in a frighteningly short time.

All backcountry skiers should obtain training in first aid. Accidents happen in uncontrolled environments, and the ability to administer the appropriate first aid can be vital in preventing a harrowing ordeal.

Skiers should always travel with a first aid kit. The contents of each kit may vary, but they should include an assortment of bandages (including a combine dressing or sanitary napkin) to control bleeding, blister prevention and repair materials, an emergency blanket, a triangular bandage, and a hypothermia thermometer. I also like to carry two Ace bandages and a lightweight flexible splint called a Sam Splint (available from The Seaberg Company, South Beach, OR 97366). They make it possible to immobilize an injured extremity quickly and get on your way—nice to be able to do when a frigid wind is nipping away at you.

Hypothermia and frostbite are the two most common winter problems. They are preventable if the early symptoms are recognized.

Hypothermia

Hypothermia is a condition in which the temperature of the body core (the area around the vital organs) drops below its normal level of 98.6 degrees.

Symptoms. Symptoms in the early stages of hypothermia include shivering, lips and fingernails becoming cyanotic (blue), mental confusion, and difficulty using the hands. The victim may become apathetic and complain of being cold. This is called mild hypothermia, when the body core temperature (taken rectally) is above 90 degrees, or the oral temperature is down to 95 degrees.

In moderate to severe hypothermia, the body core temperature is below 90 degrees (taken rectally), or the oral temperature is below 95 degrees. Symptoms include uncontrollable shivering, mental confusion and denial that there is a problem, slurred speech, and lack of coordination. Left untreated, this condition can deteriorate until the person is unresponsive, possibly unconscious, shivering has stopped, and pulse and respiration decrease.

What is going on here? The body is simply losing heat at a faster rate than it can generate it. The body loses heat in four ways: through evaporation (through breathing, for example), conduction (as happens when sitting on the snow or wearing wet clothes), radiation (from exposed skin, especially around the head and neck), and convection (as in wind chill).

The body gains heat from digesting food, engaging in physical activity, being near external heat sources such as a fire or a warm body, and shunting blood from the extremities and the skin to the body core.

Treatment. The treatment of mild hypothermia addresses how and why the body becomes cold. The basic principles of treatment for mild hypothermia are as follows:

1. Stop heat loss. Remove the victim from the cold, wet environment if possible. When far from shelter, one of the

most important steps to take is to *remove wet clothes and replace them with dry clothing*. This means removing layers of wet polypropylene as well. People who are hypothermic are generally unable to generate enough body heat to dry out their clothing, regardless of what "miracle fabrics" they are wearing. Add extra insulation over the dry layers.

2. If possible, place the victim in a warm environment. Body-to-body skin contact in a sleeping bag can be helpful but is often unnecessary if other measures are taken.

3. If the victim is conscious, give him or her warm, sweet liquids and high-energy foods, such as gorp.

Treatment of moderate to severe hypothermia is a much more complicated affair, with many experts arguing that it should only be done in hospitals. If the victim has been hypothermic for a number of hours, metabolic changes have taken place and rewarming too quickly can cause greater harm. The best option, and one that is usually feasible in the accessible New England mountains, is to evacuate the victim to a hospital with as little jostling as possible. The victim should not be given warm liquids, since that can cause blood from the body core to rush to the extremities, further depressing the victim's core temperature. The victim should be wrapped in a vapor barrier cocoon consisting of a sleeping bag, a waterproof plastic or coated nylon bag, and a reflective emergency blanket.

Prevention. It is necessary to be aware of the causes of hypothermia and heat loss in order to prevent it. A few pointers:

• Eat throughout the day when outdoors in the winter. The human body burns an enormous number of calories to stay warm in the winter. One lunch stop on the trail is inadequate. Have snack foods accessible, and stop often to snack.

• Stop evaporative heat loss by shedding layers of clothing *before* you begin sweating.

- "If your feet are cold, put on a hat." The old backpacker's saying is a wise one. Up to 75 percent of the body's total heat production can be lost through the head and neck.

- Prevent conductive heat loss by putting on a windshell *before* arriving at an exposed area such as a summit ridge.

- Drink lots of fluids.

The latter point deserves special mention. Because they may not be sweating as much as they do in the summer, people incorrectly assume that dehydration is not a problem in the winter. This is a serious mistake. The combination of perspiring while exhaling humidified air and inhaling dry winter air can dehydrate a skier rapidly. Dehydration is especially a problem for people who are overweight, since they tend to sweat more. A steady loss of body fluids makes a person more prone to frostbite and hypothermia. Signs of mild dehydration include headaches and brightly colored urine. Prevent this by ensuring that every member of the party has at least a liter of water that is accessible during the day, and make sure people are drinking. Keep your water bottle on a neck lanyard or in an inside pocket so that it is next to your body. This will keep the contents from freezing. Alcoholic beverages should be avoided. They act as a diuretic, causing further dehydration.

Frostbite

Frostbite is what happens when body tissue freezes. It can affect any part of the body, but parts that protrude are particularly susceptible. The ears, nose, fingers, and toes must be closely monitored in cold weather.

Symptoms and Treatment. There are two main types of frostbite. *Superficial frostbite* is indicated by patches of white or waxy skin that may be hard to the touch, although underlying tissue is still soft. The affected area feels numb or very cold. The treatment for superficial frostbite is to rewarm the affected body part. This can be done by placing it against warm skin, such as putting a superficially frostbitten foot in a partner's armpit or on his or her stomach, or just placing a warm hand over a numb nose or cheek. Do not rub the affected part, as this can cause deep tissue damage.

Deep frostbite is indicated by white, waxy skin over solid underlying tissue. The affected part feels totally numb, and it is difficult for the victim to move it. Field treatment for deep frostbite involves first preventing further injury. Keep the patient warm and make sure no other areas are exposed. Thawing can be done only under sterile conditions, and the affected area cannot be in any danger of refreezing or having to bear weight. Thawing out a frostbitten extremity is extremely painful. It is almost always preferable to ski or walk someone with deep frostbite out to a hospital, where comprehensive medical treatment is available. If you rewarm a foot with deep frostbite in the field, the victim will have to be carried out.

A person with deep frostbite should be evacuated as soon as possible. The victim should be fed plenty of fluids to decrease susceptibility to further injury.

Prevention. Don't wait for problems to develop. If someone is complaining of numbness or tingling in the extremities, *stop and deal with it*. Waiting "just until you get to the car" can lead to permanent damage.

Preventing frostbite should be a group effort. When skiing high on a summit ridge where the wind is blowing hard, partners should check one another continually for any white splotches on the face, ears, and nose. Other pointers to help prevent frostbite:

• Avoid tight boots. They are a prime cause of frostbitten toes. If your boots are snug, it is better to remove one layer of socks than to constrict circulation. If you have been frostbitten in the past or have poor circulation in your extremities, consider experimenting with some combination of double boots, insulated supergaiters, wool or felt boot insoles, and vapor barrier socks.

- For hands, mittens are warmer than gloves, especially when used in combination with glove or mitten liners.

- Have adequate wind protection. This includes wearing balaclavas or face masks on exposed summits.

- Constantly wiggle cold toes and fingers. Run around or do jumping jacks to increase circulation to the extremities. Keep moving.

- Avoid direct skin contact with bare metal or cooking fuel.

Rescues

If someone is hurt, you must be equipped to stabilize the situation, attempt self-rescue, and, as a last resort, go for help. When dealing with an accident, your first responsibility is to yourself and the other uninjured members of your party. You won't be much help if you get hurt jumping off a cliff after your friend just so you can reach him or her quickly. After making sure that no one else is in danger and the victim's medical condition is stabilized, you must make a decision regarding evacuation. If the victim is able to get to a trailhead without suffering further injury, that is always preferable to waiting around in the snow for a rescue party to arrive.

Time is critical in the winter. Do not waste an hour making an improvised litter if you do not think you can drag it out on your own. If you are alone with a helpless partner, you are usually better off seeking the proper equipment and enough people to perform the rescue efficiently and safely than exhausting yourself and becoming a second victim. If you go for help, be sure you know exactly where you left your partner, leaving flashing or some type of marker along the way if you are not on a trail. Bring detailed information about the victim's condition and the nature of the injury; completing the accident report form that is on the back of the AMC maps for Mount Washington and Chocorua-Waterville will provide rescuers with the most important information. This will allow the rescuers to respond in the most appropriate way and know which first aid equipment to bring. (See appendix B for emergency contact phone numbers.)

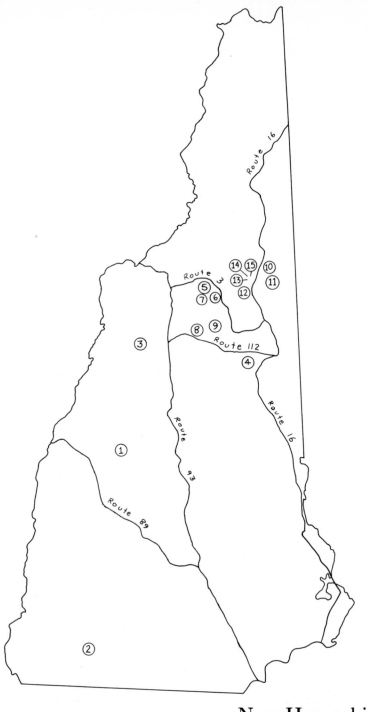

New Hampshire

Part II

NEW HAMPSHIRE

A Note on Maps. The status of USGS mapping in New Hampshire is poor. Older, out-of-date 15-minute maps have not been listed with route descriptions in this section where newer, more accurate AMC maps are available that cover the same area. In addition to the AMC maps, the DeLorme *Trail Map and Guide to the White Mountain National Forest* and the

Waumbek Books *Washington and Lafayette Trail Maps* cover all routes in this section except Mounts Cardigan and Monadnock.

Most of these maps can be purchased at sporting goods and convenience stores in the White Mountain region. See the bibliography for additional information on maps.

Mount Cardigan

THE TOURS   The Alexandria Ski Trail and the Duke's Ski Trail are classic down-mountain runs that descend the east side of the Firescrew–Mount Cardigan summit ridge to the AMC Cardigan Lodge.

LENGTH   Alexandria Ski Trail: 0.75 mile; Duke's Ski Trail: 1 mile

ELEVATION   Starting: 1,300 feet; high point: Alexandria, 2,800 feet, and Duke's Ski Trail, 2,400 feet

MAP   AMC map no. 2 (Mount Cardigan)

DIFFICULTY   More difficult

HOW TO GET THERE   From the Bristol exit on I-93, follow NH 3A west to the stone church at the foot of Newfound Lake, continue straight through the crossroad at 1.9 miles, bear right at 3.1 miles, and turn left at 6.3 miles. At 7.4 miles from the church, turn right on a gravel road, then bear right at 7.5 miles at the "Red Schoolhouse," and continue to the lodge at 8.9 miles. This road is plowed in winter but is notoriously difficult driving. Be equipped with gear (shovel, chains) to extricate your car if necessary.

The ski trails on Mount Cardigan and neighboring Firescrew are two of the more historic runs in New England. Mount Cardigan, or "Old Baldy" to the locals, was the center of activity for skiers of the Appalachian Mountain Club after

Telemarking on the narrow upper section of the Alexandria Trail.

the club purchased 500 acres and a barn on the east side of the mountain in 1934. The "Appies," as AMC members are sometimes called, quickly set about developing the slopes of Cardigan and Firescrew for downhill skiing. They took advantage of abandoned pastureland just west of the current lodge off the Manning Trail. The large slope they cleared, known as the Duke's Pasture, is still used as a main site for AMC ski clinics.

The first ski trail to be cut by AMC volunteers was the Duke's Trail on Firescrew. Firescrew gets its name from the spiraling plume of fire seen for miles around when the mountain burned in 1855. The trail was named for Duke Dimitri von Leuchtenberg, a man of Russian nobility who taught skiing at the Peckett's resort near Franconia and directed work projects for the CCC in central New Hampshire. The duke blazed the original trail, which volunteers dutifully cut in the summer of 1934. That winter the AMC hired Charles Proctor to teach skiing. A former Dartmouth and Olympic team skier, Proctor was responsible for the design of many ski trails in New Hampshire.

In 1935 the state of New Hampshire hired Proctor to lay out the Alexandria Ski Trail (named for the nearby town) for expert skiers. The CCC was brought in to provide the labor for the job, and the down-mountain trail was first skied that winter. The Kimball Ski Trail was another popular run, but it has since been abandoned. Word about the new trails spread quickly, and by 1938 the crowds flocking to Cardigan were straining the capacity of the small AMC lodge. A new lodge was built in 1939, and it is still in use today.

Ski traffic on Mount Cardigan dropped off significantly after World War II, another casualty of the many lift-served skiing opportunities nearby. The current caretaker reports that activity has once again picked up, and that the ski lodge is packed on most winter weekends. Reservations to stay at the lodge or in the adjoining house are accepted for groups of ten or more. Information on staying at Cardigan Lodge may be obtained by calling the AMC at 617-523-0636.

The trails on Cardigan are still exciting and high-quality

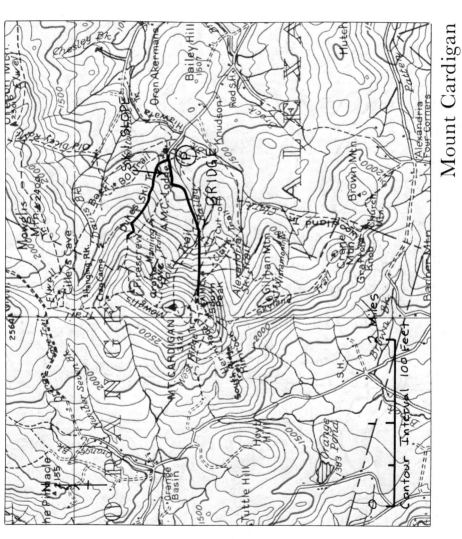

Mount Cardigan

ski runs that are maintained perennially. Leaving Cardigan Lodge and heading toward the Alexandria and Duke's trails, the slopes of the Duke's Pasture appear shortly on the right. A rope ski tow was in operation on these slopes in the early 1940s, powered by a gasoline motor from a car that several people dragged to the top of the hill. When skiing down the Duke's Trail, you can still find the remains of the engine just off to the right before you enter the clearing.

The Alexandria Ski Trail is reached after following the Holt Trail 0.8 mile, crossing a bridge over Bailey Brook, and reaching a three-way trail junction. The Alexandria Ski Trail continues straight ahead. The trail follows the fall line from just below the summit ledges and runs for about 0.75 mile. It is about 20 feet wide, a comfortable width for carving turns down the mountain.

The Alexandria has the classic qualities of the best CCC ski trails. It was designed by a skier for skiers, turning where it needs to and wide enough to have fun on. The outlooks higher up on the trail, particularly when it reaches the rocky ledges, face north and east, and offer a nice panorama of southern New Hampshire. The trail narrows at its upper reaches to about 10 feet wide and ranges in steepness from 20 to 25 degrees.

The original trail continued to the top of South Peak but now ends at the junction with the Clark Trail at Pajama Ledge, presumably because of soil erosion higher up. The rocky summit ledges of Cardigan are very exposed and plastered with ice and snow; they can be treacherous without proper climbing equipment in winter. Most skiers now simply climb the Alexandria and ski back down the same way.

The Duke's Trail is a little longer than the Alexandria and is considered somewhat easier. It is no longer as popular as the Alexandria and can be somewhat difficult to find. Starting from the ski slopes just west of the Cardigan Lodge, the bottom of the Duke's Trail follows the cut for the old rope tow up the mountain. The trail continues directly up the fall line of a rounded ridge for about a mile. It ends at the junction with the Manning Trail.

The skiing on Cardigan is not just limited to these classic down-mountain runs. There is a network of easy cross-country ski trails in the area of the lodge that newcomers to the sport will also enjoy. The gentle ski slopes near the lodge are a good place to practice your cross-country downhill technique. Information on AMC ski workshops that take place on Cardigan is available from the club (see appendix A).

The slopes of Mount Cardigan continue to offer high-quality mountain skiing, even after fifty years. As you swoosh down the Alexandria, picture the person ahead of you in 10-pound hickory skis with cable bindings, bearing down the hill and reveling in the discovery of this "new" sport called skiing. Whether it's 1939 or 1989, not much changes about that thrill of floating through deep snow down the side of a mountain with spectacular views of the New England countryside all around you.

Mount Monadnock

THE TOURS   Monadnock State Park has developed a network of moderate backcountry ski trails that crisscross the base of the mountain. They are a good introduction to backcountry skiing.

LENGTH   Loop tours from 1 mile to more than 7 miles in length can be done.

ELEVATION   Starting: 1,300 feet; high point: 1,700 feet

MAPS   USGS Monadnock Mountain (7.5-minute x 15-minute, 1984); AMC map no. 1 (Grand Monadnock). Neither topographic map shows all ski trails (and the USGS map shows them in the wrong places). Topographic maps may be used in conjunction with the free sketch map *Ski Touring Trails Around Monadnock State Park,* available at the ranger cabin next to the main parking lot at Monadnock State Park.

DIFFICULTY   Moderate

FEE $1 per person on weekends, free on weekdays

HOW TO GET THERE   From Jaffrey, take NH 124 west 2 miles to Dublin Road, and turn right at the sign for Monadnock State Park. Turn left on Poole Memorial Road just beyond the Monadnock Bible Conference. Trails begin from the parking lot at the end of the road.

Mount Monadnock has a special place in the hearts of many New Englanders. Standing alone like a beacon over southern New England, it is the gateway to the mountain

Backcountry skiing at the foot of Mount Monadnock.

ranges to the north. The mountain has been sketched and painted by numerous artists and written about by dozens of writers and poets, including Emerson and Thoreau (Thoreau actually lived high on the mountain in the mid-1800s). From its 3,165-foot summit, which is up to 2,000 feet higher than the surrounding valleys, one can see all six states of New England, the skyscrapers of Boston, and the summit of Mount Washington. This fact has not been lost on the area's summer hikers, who have reputedly made the mountain the second most climbed peak in the world, after Mount Fuji in Japan.

Mount Monadnock is an odd remnant from the glacial era, a rock formation that the ice cap failed to grind down on its impressive journey to the ocean some twenty thousand years ago. The mountain is such a striking example of a height-of-land standing alone above an upland plain that the word *monadnock* is used in geology to refer to all such phenomena. The Abenaki Indians who originally gave the peak its name were struck by the spiritual aspects of the land: the Abenaki word *monadnock* means "mountain," perhaps a supernatural or holy mountain with an exceptionally good outlook.

What make for the spectacular unobstructed views from the summit of Mount Monadnock, however, are the nemesis of skiers: exposed rocks. The mountain itself is not very ski-able. The hiking trails are typically narrow, boulder-strewn, and ledgy, and the mountain generally does not receive enough snow at lower elevations to fill in these trails sufficiently for skiing. As for the much touted summit views, they can be had only by climbing up the craggy, bald summit cone, which is glazed with ice throughout the winter. Skiers will have to swallow their pride and concede that Monadnock may simply represent the revenge of the snowshoer.

This is not meant to deter skiers from coming to Mount Monadnock. The mountain still boasts some excellent back-country skiing in the 12-mile network of ungroomed ski trails that crisscross the base of the mountain. Unlike the hiking trails on the mountain which get heavy traffic even in the winter, hikers and snowshoers (and pets, warns the ranger) are not allowed on the ski trails.

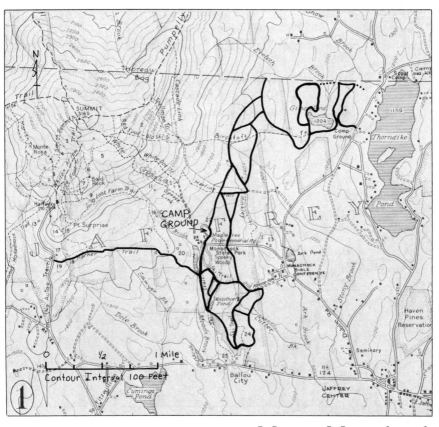

Mount Monadnock

The ski trails lie to the north and south of the parking lot next to the ranger headquarters. The trails leading to the north, which have some partial views of the mountain, leave to the right of the toilets and pass through a campground. Continue straight ahead until you come to a blue blaze marked "13" (the numbers correspond to the park's ski trail map) with an arrow pointing right; this leads to the trail network and Gilson Pond. The trail passes through a number of nice open clearings. Trail 19 is a particularly enjoyable run with a long downhill. A worthwhile day trip that takes in some of the nicest landscape in the area is the loop that can be made from the park headquarters to Gilson Pond. This tour through open forest and birch stands, and to the mountain pond from which there are views of the Pumpelly Ridge, is a well-rounded and classic day of New England woods skiing.

The trails south of the parking lot tend to be the easiest and most likely to be skiable with little snow. After an initial drop, these trails travel through marshes and fields. The stretch between junctions 2 and 4 offers the nicest view of the mountain.

The ski trails in Mount Monadnock State Park are ideal for providing novice to intermediate skiers with a taste of what backcountry skiing is all about. Only ninety minutes from Boston, it may be the perfect place for urban skiers to head just after a storm in order to sample some bona fide New England powder. This proximity, however, means you may have competition. The ranger notes that his 150-car lot often fills on weekends, although it is usually empty midweek.

Other Options. The Wapack Trail is a skyline trail following the ridgecrest of the Wapack Range. It extends for 21 miles from Ashburnham, Massachusetts, to Pack Monadnock Mountain. It was originally designed as a ski trail and can be skied in several sections. Details and a map may be found in the *AMC White Mountain Guide.*

Mount Moosilauke

THE TOURS   The Snapper Ski Trail and the Carriage Road were two of the original sites for eastern championship ski races in the 1930s. The Moosilauke summit cone is also flanked by large skiable snowfields.

LENGTH   Carriage Road to Snapper Trail, 3.1 miles; Carriage Road to summit, 5.1 miles; Snapper Trail, 1 mile

ELEVATION   Starting: 1,700 feet; top of Snapper: 3,400 feet; summit: 4,802 feet

MAPS   USGS Mount Moosilauke (7.5-minute series, 1967) and USGS Mount Kineo (7.5-minute series, 1973); AMC map no. 5 (Franconia)

DIFFICULTY   Carriage Road: more difficult; Snapper Trail: most difficult

HOW TO GET THERE   From I-93, take the North Woodstock exit to NH 112. Go west on NH 112, then west on NH 118. The Ravine Lodge Road is on the north side of NH 118, 7.2 miles west of the junction with NH 112. To get to the Carriage Road trailhead, drive 3 miles west on NH 118 beyond the Ravine Lodge Road and turn right at a small bridge. The Moosilauke Inn and Breezy Point are 1.6 miles up the road. Take care not to block driveways or the road when parking.

Mount Moosilauke (there is a debate over whether the peak's name is pronounced "Moosi-locky" or "Moosi-lock") has some of the richest early ski history of any of the White

Descending the snow-capped summit cone of Mount Moosilauke.

Mountains. At 4,802 feet, it is the westernmost 4,000-footer in the Whites. The summit itself is the high point on a long cirque-shaped ridge which includes three other summits over 4,000 feet.

The history of Moosilauke is intimately tied up with the history of the Dartmouth Outing Club (DOC). The DOC began purchasing tracts of land on Moosilauke in 1920 and now owns more than 2,200 acres on the mountain. DOC skiers were a major force in New England ski history, in part because of their activities on Moosilauke. They were greatly assisted by the legendary German ski coach Otto Schniebs when they hired him in 1930. Schniebs advised the Dartmouth skiers to abandon their stiff, upright skiing style and adopt the style pioneered by Hannes Schneider at his renowned Arlberg ski school in Austria. This "called for a low crouch, an up-and-down motion, skis apart in the stem position, and use of poles. The graceful telemark went into eclipse," writes Allen Adler in his excellent book *New England & Thereabouts—A Ski Tracing*.

A popular anecdote about Schniebs, which has often been retold, comes from a talk he gave in Boston. As described in the *American Ski Annual*, Schniebs was posed with a difficult question:

> "Otto," asked a bright-eyed young lady who had the look of one haunted by a deep problem, "what would you do if you were coming down a steep narrow trail a little too fast and there were stumps and trees and ice and things all around?" "Vell [replied Schniebs], either take the damned skis off und valk—or schtem—schtem like Hell!"

Together, the DOC and Mount Moosilauke are responsible for a number of notable firsts in ski history. The first organized downhill race in the United States took place on the Mount Moosilauke Carriage Road in April 1927. Called the Moosilauke Down Mountain Race, it had about fifteen entrants. The race started at the junction of the Carriage Road

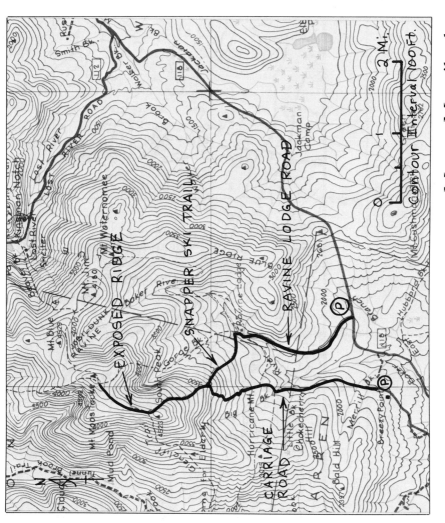

Mount Moosilauke

and the Glencliff Trail; it was won by Charles Proctor with a time of 21 minutes. It was also the site of the first invitational club ski races in 1931. In March 1933 the Carriage Road was the site of the first U.S. National Downhill Championships. The race was won in 8 minutes by DOC skier Henry ("Bem") Woods, with classmate Harry Hillman (of Hillman Highway fame in Tuckerman Ravine) coming in a close second.

Al Sise raced in that first championship. He recalled in a personal interview, "Nobody ever thought of course preparation back then. There were big drifts on the trail, and I flew off one of those and landed on something soft. It turned out to be the guy who started in front of me." Sise explained that in other races "the guy who fell the least number of times—say, less than twelve—won on Carriage Road races. As Alex Bright used to say, 'If you didn't fall, it was a sure sign you weren't skiing fast enough.'"

Just before the national championship in 1933, the first race on the Richard Taft Trail on Cannon Mountain was run. Compared with the narrow Carriage Road with its many switchbacks, the Taft was wide open and steeper. "Those who correctly interpreted this development knew that the future of downhill racing lay on that kind of trail and that the Carriage Road was obsolete," wrote David Hooke in his history of the DOC, *Reaching That Peak*. Dartmouth skiers were determined to have a trail that kept them and their mountain at the forefront of skiing. This led Coach Schniebs to design Hell's Highway, the most famous—and feared—ski trail to grace the side of Mount Moosilauke.

Hell's Highway was cut by Dartmouth students in the summer of 1933. It started from just below South Peak, descending the steep west side of Gorge Brook Ravine to Gorge Brook, where it followed what is now the Gorge Brook Trail to the Ravine Lodge. The result was a trail that was described in a 1939 guidebook to skiing in the East as "the steepest and most difficult trail in New England, requiring expert technique." The upper part of the trail dropped 900 feet in a half mile, including the famous 38-degree section known as the "Rock Garden." The steepness of Hell's Highway was to be its undoing: the devastating 1938 hurricane caused a landslide on the Rock Garden, and the resulting sections of exposed bedrock never again held snow. The trail quickly disappeared into ski lore. The approximate route of Hell's Highway can be followed today by hiking the abandoned Slide Trail, which goes from the Gorge Brook Trail to the Carriage Road, just before its junction with the Glencliff Trail. The loss of Hell's Highway prompted the DOC to search for new terrain for skiing. The result was the construction of the Dipper and Snapper ski trails in 1939, of which only the latter still exists. "Snapper" was the nickname of Ed Wells, a well-known DOC skier who was involved in designing the trail. It referred to his terse but wise contributions during the nightly bull sessions of the trail crew. The Snapper was primarily a recreational trail, although a few races were held on it.

The skiing on Mount Moosilauke is no longer as sought after as it once was. The Snapper Trail has grown in considerably, making it an enjoyable run for only the best skiers. Snowmobilers now regularly travel the Carriage Road to the summit, and the trail has also grown in somewhat. But Moosilauke remains a classic ski tour for other reasons. It is a mountain rich in ski history and offers one of the most dramatic landscapes for skiing. Skiing up its exposed summit ridge is an exciting alpine experience. Skiers will frequently enjoy a mild climb up, only to battle a raging wind once they break out of the trees in the final push for the summit. Good judgment is required to determine how to reach the summit in such conditions, or whether to proceed at all. Those climbing to the summit should consider skirting the summit cone to one side to avoid catching the full force of the weather.

It is said that Otto Schniebs was lured to the United States on the promise that the nation had good skiing. Upon being brought to Mount Moosilauke, he was appalled at the small size of the mountain in comparison with his Austrian Alps. His attitude changed when he hiked the mountain and was forced to crawl on his hands and knees along the summit ridge because of the ferocious weather.

Perhaps the most dramatic part of the ski experience on Moosilauke is this summit itself. A bald, windswept summit cone caps the mountain. Skiers can climb up and carve turns for several hundred feet below the summit, taking in panoramic views of successive ridges of the White Mountains to the east and the Connecticut Valley and the Green Mountains to the west. Summit snow conditions can be tricky. You may be skiing on top of windblown crust one minute, bouncing over *sastrugi* (the fragile, rippled snow patterns that grow into the wind) the next, and end up in feathery powder as you traverse through a protected pocket where snow has eddied. Skiers should be aware that a fall high on the summit cone can result in a fast and uncontrollable slide down into the trees. Skiers should take care to ski where there is a forgiving run-out or be proficient at self-arresting after a fall.

The two classic ski tours on Moosilauke are the Carriage Road and the Snapper Trail.

The Carriage Road may be approached in two ways. The first is via the unplowed Ravine Lodge Road. The road leaves NH 118 on the north side, 7.2 miles west of its junction with NH 112 just outside of North Woodstock, or 5.8 miles east of its northerly junction with NH 25. There is room to park at the beginning of the Ravine Lodge Road; it is a 1.6-mile ski to the lodge from NH 118. The Ravine Lodge, owned by the DOC, is closed in the winter.

From the lodge, skiers may follow the Gorge Brook Trail for 0.2 mile to where the Hurricane Trail branches off to the left. It is one mile to the Carriage Road from here. It is preferable to avoid skiing up the Snapper Trail to where it joins the Carriage Road, both because it is a steep climb and out of courtesy to other skiers. The Snapper is considerably more enjoyable as an untracked powder run than as a survival ski course that has been rutted and broken up by the tracks of thoughtless ascending skiers.

A slightly more direct approach to the Carriage Road that follows its original path begins from Breezy Point, the site of the old Moosilauke Inn. The road to Breezy Point leaves NH 118 2.5 miles from its junction with NH 25, or 3.3 miles west of the Ravine Lodge Road turnout. It is 1.6 miles to the end of the Breezy Point Road, where you may park along the side of the road. The Carriage Road is an obvious, wide path that begins where the plowed road ends. It will most likely have snowmobile tracks. The trail ascends moderately for the first 1.5 miles, then begins climbing more steeply.

The series of switchbacks in the Carriage Road were the source of a humorous event that took place during the U.S. National Downhill Championship Race in 1933. Some of the bolder skiers realized that they could save time by cutting through the woods and eliminating some of the broad turns at the bottom. The brothers Leonard and Hollis Phillips, fresh from training at the Hannes Schneider ski school in Austria, were determined to win the race. They had their father stand at the opening of the cutoff path that they had blazed when they climbed up; he held a long branch in front of the detour so other skiers could not use it. When his sons came by, he swiftly stepped aside, allowing them to fly through the trees and save time. Despite these efforts, however, neither brother won the race.

The Carriage Road is not particularly scenic at lower elevations, where it passes through second-growth hardwood forests. The path intersects with the Snapper 3.1 miles from Breezy Point. From here, it is 2 miles to the summit. The final mile follows a pronounced ridge above treeline, with excellent views in all directions. This section should not be attempted in poor or deteriorating weather conditions, since there is no quick escape from the ridge.

The Carriage Road is only about 10 feet wide, with closely spaced firs lining the sides in the upper sections just below the ridge. The downhill run doesn't allow for much finesse until you near the end. You can either snowplow, or, as some skiers have opted to do, just keep your climbing skins on and enjoy the ride.

The Snapper Ski Trail leaves the Carriage Road about three-quarters of a mile above where the Hurricane Trail enters from the Ravine Lodge. The top of the trail is obvious, marked by no fewer than four signs. Dropping 1,000 feet in its

1.2-mile length, the Snapper is a thrilling run in good snow conditions. The upper section of the trail is only 6–8 feet wide and drops steeply. The young birch trees lining the trail are evidence that the Snapper was once considerably wider but has grown in during the years that skiers have neglected it. Skiing it demands quick maneuvering and rapid, tight turns.

After about 0.3 mile, the trail opens up somewhat, allowing for wider turns and skiing through the trees. The steep grade is fairly sustained for its entire length. Close to where it joins the Gorge Brook Trail are several stream crossings that may be open in the spring. In powder conditions, the Snapper is a satisfying and challenging trail for expert skiers. But as with many routes of comparable difficulty, crusty or icy conditions can make this route a test of survival skiing abilities.

Mount Chocorua

THE TOUR   The Champney Falls Trail climbs to the rocky summit of this peak, which dominates views of the White Mountains from the southeast. The trail passes the beautiful Champney Falls and follows an old logging road, which is an enjoyable descent route.

LENGTH   3.6 miles to summit

ELEVATION   Starting: 1,300 feet; high point: 3,475 feet

MAPS   AMC map no. 4 (Chocorua-Waterville)

DIFFICULTY   More difficult

HOW TO GET THERE   The Champney Falls trailhead parking lot is marked by a brown USFS sign on the Kancamagus Highway (NH 112), 11.5 miles west of NH 16 in Conway.

Mount Chocorua is distinctive as a ski tour because of its dramatic alpine quality. Chocorua is a 3,475-foot peak renowned for its craggy summit. It is said to be the most photographed of all the White Mountains, more closely resembling a peak one might find near the Matterhorn than amongst the characteristic White Mountain glacial domes.

Chocorua is also a mountain steeped in colorful history. The legend told about the mountain is a mixture of folklore and fact, leaving future generations to discern one from the other. The mountain was named for the Sokosis Indian chief

A skier stops to admire Champney Falls on his way up Mount Chocorua.

Chocorua, who died on the mountain that now bears his name. That much is not disputed. It is the question of *how* Chocorua died that inflames passion.

One story has it that Chocorua entrusted the care of his son to a local settler named Cornelius Campbell while he traveled to Canada "to consult with his people." Chocorua had enjoyed good relations with the white settlers, and Campbell is said to have been a friend. But Chocorua's son supposedly ingested some fox poison by accident and died. Upon discovering this tragedy, Chocorua slew Campbell's wife and children for revenge. Campbell is said then to have pursued Chocorua to the summit of the mountain, where, just before being shot by Campbell, the Indian chief declared, "Chocorua goes to the Great Spirit—his curse stays with the white man."

Another popular version of the story says that Chocorua's son was not involved at all. White settlers, enraged by an Indian massacre that allegedly occurred in the area, chased Chocorua to the top of the mountain where he leaped to his death. Several paintings depict Chocorua on a prominent summit boulder on the verge of death. Today's backcountry skiers can retrace the summit climb and let their minds wander as they survey the landscape and imagine the events that have now been immortalized in many songs, paintings, and stories.

The Champney Falls Trail is a popular summer hiking route up Chocorua, and it is wide enough to be an enjoyable ski trail. The route ascends a mildly graded logging road that is well marked with yellow blazes. After about half a mile, the trail climbs up onto the shoulder of Champney Brook via a sharp turn—to be taken note of for the descent. The route soon rejoins the logging road and continues to a trail junction, at 1.4 miles, with a loop trail that drops down slightly to Champney Falls and Pitcher Falls.

The half-mile detour to the falls is well worth it. Champney Falls resembles a small box canyon, appearing curiously on the northern flanks of the mountain. It looks as if the bedrock simply broke apart, the water caught frozen in time spilling over the lip of the vertical wall. Watch out for slush and water

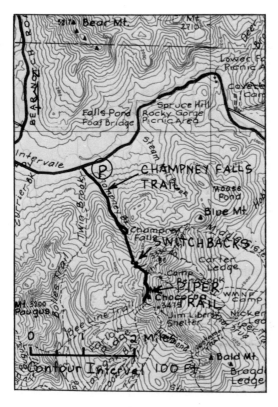

Mount Chocorua

beneath the falls as you ski around taking in the sights. To rejoin the main path at the end of the loop, it will be necessary for you to remove your skis and scramble up a steep, rocky section of trail.

The trail to the summit continues up the western shoulder of the now deepening ravine formed by Champney Brook. The trail has a number of drainage divots, including one where the remains of the telephone wire that led to the now defunct fire tower on the Middle Sister can be seen sticking out of the snow. At 2.4 miles, the trail begins traversing across the headwall of the ravine via several long, sharp switchbacks. Looking behind you at the first right turn, you will see the deep drainage fall away to provide dramatic views to the northwest of the Pemigewasset Wilderness.

After a half mile of climbing the switchbacks, the route comes to the first of several trail junctions. At the first junction, a trail diverges left to the Middle Sister, one of three "sister" peaks that form the long ridge running northeast from the summit of Mount Chocorua. The Champney Falls Trail continues up a narrow, winding chute toward a treeless knoll. Here you have your first unobstructed view of the rocky summit cone. It is a striking view looking south: the peak is backlit by the sun, which often has the effect of creating a rainbow shroud around the windy summit rocks. Several trail signs here direct you to the Piper Trail, which brings you the final 0.6 mile to the summit.

But the ski tour doesn't just end with a shuffle on up the trail. The real excitement starts about a quarter mile from the summit itself, where trees meet rock, and skis must come off. After you take a break to snack and put on wind protection, the mountaineering element of this tour comes into its own. For those planning to continue to the summit, the final leg will require kicking steps into the wind-crusted snow. Climbers must be extremely careful of rime, which plasters the rocks. Upon reaching the area right below the summit rock itself, you will have two options. The top can be attained by easy scrambling around to the right, or if you prefer to reach the summit with a flourish, you can jam up a final 10-foot icy crack that tops out right at the USGS bench mark.

The summit views on Chocorua are famous for good reason: a 360-degree panorama is the reward for your efforts. The huge boulder that sits off the northeastern corner of the summit rock is presumably the one appearing in so many paintings and drawings of the final moments in the life of Chocorua.

Descending from where you left your skis, it is best to keep climbing skins on until you return to the small knoll a half mile below the summit, since the Piper Trail does some climbing until that point. From the knoll, the most challenging part of the descent is the next half mile. The narrow chute that leads back to the switchbacks is the route down. Unless you have a reliable quick turn you may opt to keep your skins on until the next trail junction a few minutes away. The descent on the Champney Falls Trail begins with three or four 120-degree switchback corners and then becomes more moderate. The open forest on the left provides abundant telemarking opportunities, and the trail itself is wide enough to link turns for several miles.

Chocorua is a wonderful introduction to the joys of mountain skiing in the White Mountains. Its combination of high-quality ski terrain, spectacular views, and the exciting summit pitch make this a classic ski mountaineering adventure.

Other Options. Possibilities for other routes on Chocorua include a loop tour that ascends the peak via the Steam Mill Brook Trail and descends the Champney Falls Trail. The former trail is not maintained but is still recognizably blazed. The Bolles Trail, which climbs to the saddle between Mounts Chocorua and Paugus, is an old tote road with a slight grade which is suitable as an easy tour in itself. For those willing to shuttle cars, a recommended continuous route over Chocorua could link up with the Liberty Trail, a moderate trail up a wide valley. Numerous other possibilities exist for skiing the trails on the southeast and southwest sides of the peak.

Pemigewasset Wilderness Region

The area in and around the Pemigewasset Wilderness is home to some of the most scenic and isolated backcountry skiing in New England. The official Pemigewasset Wilderness Area consists of 45,000 acres of designated wilderness. It is one of the few places in New England in which multiday ski trips can be undertaken without crossing roads. The possibilities for long ski tours in this area are numerous. Skiers can link day after day of high-quality touring and still not come close to exhausting the region's potential.

The highlights of skiing in "the Pemi" include gaining access to high mountain ponds that are hardly ever visited in the winter; spectacular views of the Franconia Ridge to the east and the Presidential Range to the north; and a sense of isolation that is rarely found elsewhere in the heavily traveled mountains of the Northeast. All this is complemented by the fact that the quality of the skiing in the Pemi is exceptional—for the most unlikely reason.

Ironically, the trails of the Pemi offer such good skiing because they were once the access routes for zealous loggers who ravaged the region at the turn of the century. Skiing along the Thoreau Falls Trail or the Shoal Pond Trail, observant skiers may notice that the trees on the parallel-sided paths would not grow as they do by accident. The first time I skied down the tunnel-like passageways, I could not help but notice that it was like skiing down railroad tracks, a resemblance I dismissed as ridiculous. But my mind's eye was right: the Pemigewasset Wilderness was indeed once crisscrossed by miles of railroad tracks built by logging tycoons. The story of these early lumbermen and their wilderness railroad empires is told in fascinating detail by Francis Belcher in his book *Logging Railroads of the White Mountains*.

The Zealand valley and the Pemigewasset River valley quickly caught the eye of J. E. Henry, the most famous and colorful logging boss in New Hampshire history. In 1884 Henry opened the Zealand Valley Railroad, which plied the route now covered by the Zealand Road (FR 16) from NH 302 all the way through Zealand Notch to Shoal Pond—a distance of more than 10 miles. Henry employed up to 250 people, housing them in small villages established deep in the woods of the Zealand valley. Little now remains of these logging camps besides clearings. Even the town of Zealand, a bustling center of business just west of the current Zealand Campground, which once had its own post office, has disappeared without a trace.

Henry's legacy in the Zealand valley was one of natural devastation. Beginning in 1886, large quantities of slash caused the first of several catastrophic fires that swept through the valley all the way up the slopes of Whitewall and Zealand mountains. The clear-cutting and fires prompted one writer to dub the area "Death Valley" early in this century. Belcher quotes an 1892 newspaper editorial from the Boston *Transcript*:

> The beautiful Zealand Valley is one vast scene of waste and desolation; immense heaps of sawdust roll down the slopes to choke the stream and, by the destructive acids distilled from their decaying substance, to poison the fish; smoke rises night and day from fires which are maintained to destroy the still accumulating piles of slabs and other mill debris.

The ecological recovery of the Zealand valley is nothing short of remarkable. Along the trail to the AMC Zealand Falls Hut today, the forest has regenerated with birches and other second-growth trees, and the area is now home to the largest lynx population in the state. Evidence of the destruction that once reigned there has not been erased, but it is no longer the blight it once was.

Henry's attention was brought next to the vast lumbering opportunities that lay just south of Zealand Notch in the

Pemigewasset valley. In the mid-1890s, Henry began focusing his efforts on penetrating this virgin wilderness. Once again, the chosen means of transporting people and lumber was the railroad. Henry oversaw the construction of rail lines from what is now the Kancamagus Highway (NH 112) that ran north alongside the East Branch of the Pemigewasset River to 13 Falls, and east over what is now the Wilderness Trail to beyond Stillwater Junction. Logging trains would normally make two round-trips a day between Lincoln and the logging camps. In the summer, a fare of seventy-five cents was charged to bring tourists in to see the vast logging operations. Belcher quotes from a 1926 book:

> On gala days in the height of the summer season two or three flat cars used to be rigged up with extemporized railings and filled with chairs, and a hundred or more excursionists made the trip up into "Henry's Woods," to wonder at the new mountains and valleys, exclaim over the winding road, marvel at the various camps, and raid the cook's quarters for hot doughnuts.

For all that may rightly be said about the destruction wrought by Henry, skiers will appreciate that his rights-of-way endure as a well-constructed bed for the trails on which they now ski. As Belcher notes, "Even today the drainage ditches along these sections are doing a fine job of handling rainfall runoff. . . . Past, present, and future trampers [and skiers!] in these areas stride along easily where Henry's laborers sweated profusely for his avenue to a fortune."

The tours described here are by no means the only "classic" routes in the Pemi. They represent a sampling of the high quality of skiing and the unique aesthetics of the area, covering a full range of difficulty. Some of the routes are most easily done from a base camp either at the AMC Zealand Falls Hut or from a campsite, while others can be comfortably done in a day from a trailhead.

A Note on Maps. The best map of the Pemigewasset Wilderness region, including all the tours described in this section, is AMC map no. 5 (Franconia). It is preferable to use a recent edition of this map, because some trails have been rerouted since the 1960s.

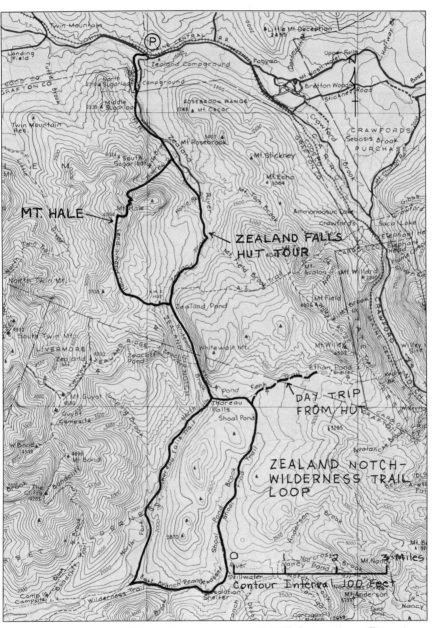

Pemigewasset Wilderness Region

Zealand Falls Hut Tour
Zealand Notch-Wilderness Trail Loop
Mount Hale

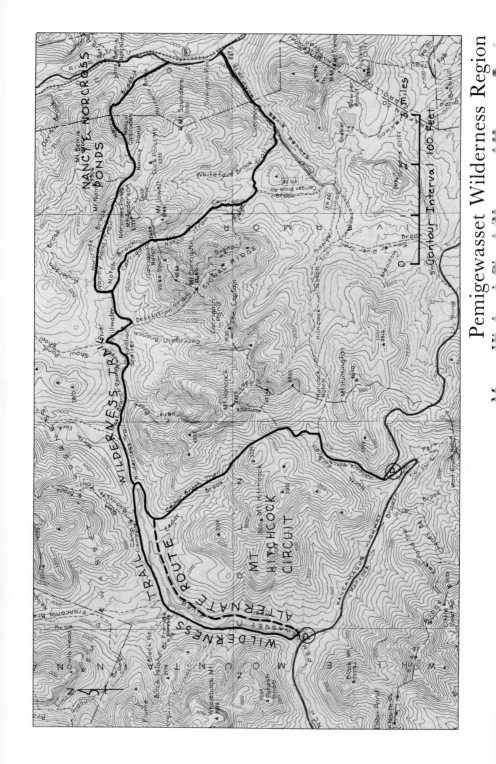

Pemigewasset Wilderness Region

Pemigewasset Wilderness Region

Zealand Falls Hut Tour

THE TOUR   The Spruce Goose Trail from NH 302 leads to the Zealand Trail, which goes to the AMC Zealand Falls Hut.

LENGTH   6.8 miles to the hut

ELEVATION   Starting: 1,500 feet; high point: 2,700 feet

MAPS   AMC map no. 5 (Franconia); U.S. Forest Service sketch map, *Cross Country Skiing–Snowmobiling: Zealand Valley Trails,* usually available at trailhead sign

DIFFICULTY   Moderate

HOW TO GET THERE   From the junction of NH 3 and 302 in the town of Twin Mountain, drive east 2.3 miles to a sign for the Zealand Campground on the right. Parking is in a plowed lot on the north side of the road. The route begins on the unplowed Zealand Road (FR 16), which has a large metal gate across it.

A ski trip to the AMC Zealand Falls Hut is one of the best of the few hut tours in New England. The AMC Zealand Falls Hut is one of only two AMC mountain huts that is open in the winter (see the section on Carter Dome for a description of the other one). From the hut, skiers have easy access to a number of excellent day trips that travel deep into the Pe-

A skier looking south through Zealand Notch, just beyond the Zealand Falls Hut.

migewasset Wilderness. The hut may be used as a base for a day trip, or as one stop on a multiday ski trip through the Pemi.

The concept of hut-to-hut travel in the winter has unfortunately never been developed in New England. Huts have long been the preferred means of mountain lodging in Europe. The tradition is only now catching on in the United States, where several hut-to-hut ski routes have been built in the West since the early 1980s. The benefits to the skier of hut hopping are, of course, many: being able to travel with light packs for several days while covering long distances, gaining access to remote wilderness, and meeting other winter travelers who can offer ideas and suggestions on interesting routes to seek out. New England winter mountaineers will have to content themselves with just the tantalizing taste of this experience provided by the Zealand Falls Hut, but the setting will not disappoint.

The route to the hut begins on the Zealand Road, which is used heavily in the winter as a snowmobile thoroughfare. Skiers exit to the right off the road within several hundred feet (just after the first bridge) onto the blue-blazed Spruce Goose Ski Trail. This trail was constructed in 1977 by the Young Adult Conservation Corps so that skiers and snowmobilers could be separated. The trail winds its way through the woods parallel to the road, about 600 feet away. However, the drone of snowmobile engines is still a constant backdrop to the skiing for the first 4.1 miles, particularly on weekends. The Spruce Goose Ski Trail is also not one of the most aesthetic trails, crossing as it does through a number of recently logged areas.

At 0.8 mile from the start, the trail passes through the Sugarloaf II campground. Bear around to the right side of the campground, and the Spruce Goose continues into the woods at the second "Trestle Trail" sign on the right. Shortly after the campground, the trail joins the Zealand Road for several hundred feet in order to cross the Zealand River on a bridge, reentering the woods on the right just beyond the bridge. The trail continues on easy, rolling woods terrain, before ending at

the Zealand Campground. From here, the Zealand Trail continues 2.7 miles to the hut, following the old railroad grade for
about a mile. The trail passes alternately through tunnels of
birch and tall, sparsely wooded second-growth forest. Zealand Notch comes into view as the trail winds around beaver
ponds and open meadows, evidence of the wildlife that has
repopulated the area.

The AMC Zealand Falls Hut lies at the top of a small hill
just west of the trail. The hut was built in 1932 and was
renovated in the mid-1980s. It was intended to link the western AMC huts with those in the Presidential Range to the
northwest. It gets its name from the cascades on Whitewall
Brook which are just below the hut.

Pemigewasset Wilderness Region

Zealand Notch–Wilderness Trail Loop

THE TOUR A loop tour from the AMC Zealand Falls Hut through Zealand Notch down to the East Branch of the Pemigewasset River

LENGTH 15 miles round-trip (approximately)

ELEVATION Starting: 2,700 feet; low point: 1,800 feet

MAP AMC map no. 5 (Franconia)

DIFFICULTY Moderate

HOW TO GET THERE The route can be accessed from Zealand Falls Hut (see description of Zealand Falls Hut Tour) or from the Wilderness Trail (see Mount Hitchcock Circuit description).

Zealand Notch is one of the more spectacular land formations in the White Mountains. It was once a V-shaped stream-eroded valley, but the ice sheets that once covered New England gouged their way down to the ocean and left Zealand Notch with the characteristic U-shape of glacial valleys that it now has. The notch becomes more and more impressive as you enter it. The steep rock walls of Whitewall

Skiing across Shoal Pond towards Zealand Notch.

Mountain jut overhead to the north, the blocky refuse of the glacier lies strewn about the valley floor, and the tree-covered slopes of Zealand Mountain rise to the south. A typical ski tour through the notch will usually involve stopping every few minutes just to marvel at the views.

One of the classic ski tours of the White Mountains is the trip through the notch to Thoreau Falls and down to the Pemigewasset River. This is a long tour, but the terrain is gentle enough that strong skiers will enjoy the extended stretches of kick-and-glide skiing. If your party will be breaking trail just after a big storm, it may be overly ambitious to try to cover the whole route in a day. In any case, you will need an early start to complete the whole tour in daylight.

From the Zealand Falls Hut, the Ethan Pond Trail follows the old railroad bed of J. H. Henry's Zealand Valley Railroad into the notch. The trail contours at 2,500 feet along the sparsely vegetated sides of Whitewall Mountain, the name of which presumably derives from the chalky color of the cliffs on its flank. Old scars from the huge fires that swept through here at the turn of the century are still visible on the rocks. The trail offers clear views of Mount Hale and the Hancock-Carrigain ridge and glimpses of the expanse of wilderness that lies just beyond the southern end of the notch.

Skiing across the steep slopes of Whitewall Mountain can be disconcerting if the snow is icy or crusty. The trail narrows to about 3 feet in width in places and drops off rather steeply, keeping you on your edges on some exposed sections.

From the southern end of the notch, the best way to ski the loop is to descend the Shoal Pond Trail to the Wilderness Trail and return on the Thoreau Falls Trail. Most of the vertical drop on the latter trail is lost in the first half mile south of Thoreau Falls and is too steep and narrow for enjoyable skiing. The Shoal Pond Trail drops gradually over its 4.3-mile length, making for a relatively effortless cruise. Trail signs clearly mark the way all along this route.

Shoal Pond is an isolated mountain pond at about 2,500 feet. High ponds are some of the most special places in the mountains. After skiing through the woods, the sensation of coming out onto a long, white, empty clearing with expansive views of Mounts Carrigain and Hancock is breathtaking. Coming across a place like this gives one a feeling of having sampled a full palette of wilderness treats.

Traveling down the Shoal Pond Trail is one of the best ways to experience skiing the old railroad beds. The Zealand Valley Railroad came down through Zealand Notch all the way to Shoal Pond, with a spur to Ethan Pond. From the early 1900s until the 1920s, the East Branch & Lincoln Railroad was making two round-trips a day between Lincoln and Camp 21, which was located on Shoal Pond Brook about a mile north of Stillwater Junction. The tracks continued a half mile north of the camp to Labrador Brook.

The ski tour continues through Stillwater Junction, once a major switching point and river crossing for the logging trains. Bearing east on the Wilderness Trail, it is 2.6 miles to the junction of the Thoreau Falls Trail. The Thoreau Falls Trail is flat for most of its length, traveling down some of the abandoned rail beds on the east side of the North Fork of the Pemigewasset River. Two major logging camps were once located on this route, although most of the tracks were on the opposite side of the river from where the trail is now. The only trace of the activity that once thrived here can be seen in the scattered remains of bridge abutments along the river. The trail climbs up steeply just before Thoreau Falls. The falls itself is an icy, snow-covered cascade that drops off precipitously, providing a sweeping view of Mount Bond, Mount Guyot, and the Zealand Ridge.

The classic quality of this ski tour lies in the variety of terrain covered. Mountain ponds, abandoned railroads, babbling brooks, wide rivers, and waterfalls create an amazing array of scenery for one tour. The skiing, thanks to the logging tycoons, is excellent. And unlike other routes that start and end at a highway trailhead, skiing in the Pemi is a true wilderness experience. Long, uninterrupted views of mountain peaks which stretch on for miles are not part of many New England ski tours. This trip to the heart of the Pemi is a chance to see the White Mountains at their wildest.

Other Options. Shorter versions of this trip can be taken, such as going through Zealand Notch just to Shoal Pond or Thoreau Falls. The trip through the notch to Ethan Pond is another shorter (9.6 miles round-trip from the hut) alternate day trip. It is a popular and pleasant tour.

Pemigewasset Wilderness Region

Mount Hale

THE TOUR   A ski ascent of 4,054-foot Mount Hale on the Hale Brook Trail, just north of the Pemigewasset Wilderness

LENGTH   9.4 miles round-trip from Zealand Road (NH 302) trailhead up and back on the Hale Brook Trail; 14.3 miles from Zealand Road trailhead via AMC Zealand Falls Hut, the Lend-a-Hand Trail, and the Hale Brook Trail

ELEVATION   Starting (NH 302): 1,500 feet; high point: 4,054 feet

MAP   AMC map no. 5 (Franconia)

DIFFICULTY   Most difficult

HOW TO GET THERE   From the Zealand Road/NH 302 trailhead, ski in 2.5 miles on the Spruce Goose Ski Trail. Spruce Goose crosses Hale Brook, and shortly thereafter the Hale Brook Trail climbs up fairly steeply to the right (west).

From its bald, rocky summit, Mount Hale has spectacular views over the ranges of the White Mountains, from the peaks and valleys of the Pemigewasset Wilderness to the south, all the way to the Presidential Range in the north. Early fire wardens recognized that the mountain had a unique vantage

Skis come off for climbing a steep section of the Lend-a-Hand Trail on the way to the Mount Hale summit.

point, and evidence of an old fire tower can still be seen on the summit. The mountain gets its name from the Rev. Edward Everett Hale, who authored the short story "Man Without a Country" and was a frequent explorer of the White Mountains in the 1800s.

For skiers interested in doing a loop tour that returns from the Zealand Falls Hut via a route other than the more heavily used Spruce Goose Ski Trail, skiing Mount Hale will provide a challenging alternative.

Those wishing to ski Mount Hale as a day trip are best off starting from NH 302 and climbing and descending the Hale Brook Trail. If you are making the climb from the Zealand Falls Hut, the best access is the Lend-a-Hand Trail. From the hut, climb around back on the Twinway for a short distance to where the Lend-a-Hand diverges right. It is 2.7 miles to the Mount Hale summit from this junction. Within a half mile of steady but gradual climbing, the trail enters a large, open birch glade. The glade begs to be skied and is a favorite playground of the hut keepers. The trail climbs gradually until attaining the ridge that runs south off the Hale summit. The ridge has occasional open ledges and views, and a few very steep pitches that are negotiated most easily by removing skis if the snow is not too deep.

From the panoramic summit of Mount Hale, the Hale Brook Trail drops off steeply to the east. The trail is narrow at first, but it soon enters some open birch stands and begins some long switchbacks that traverse across steep slopes. The grade gradually lessens, but the trail never gets much wider than about 20 feet. The route demands an ability to link quick turns in a confined space or to be proficient at checking your speed without the option of wide, sweeping turns. The trail ends where it crosses the Spruce Goose Trail (unmarked, but obvious). From this junction it is 2.5 miles back to NH 302.

The descent of Mount Hale is a favorite among a small group of avid White Mountain skiers. The route is very lightly traveled in winter by either snowshoers or skiers, partly because of its remoteness and difficulty. This ski tour is for strong skiers, and a party should have gear along to deal with the unexpected. The reward of journeying to where others don't go is that this is typically a reliable powder run, even when other trails have only a light snow cover.

Other Options. Other challenging ski tours in the area are the Garfield Trail on Mount Garfield and the Skookumchuck Trail on Mount Lafayette.

Pemigewasset Wilderness Region
Mount Hitchcock Circuit

THE TOUR   A loop tour starting on the Kancamagus Highway (NH 112) on the Hancock Notch Trail, going to the Cedar Brook Trail and returning on the Wilderness Trail

LENGTH   13.2 miles

ELEVATION   Starting: 2,100 feet; high point: 3,100 feet; ending: 1,200 feet

MAP   AMC map no. 5 (Franconia)

DIFFICULTY   Moderate

HOW TO GET THERE   The Wilderness Trail trailhead is located at a large parking lot 4.1 miles east of the information center off the I-93 exit in Lincoln. The Hancock Notch trailhead is 5 miles east of this parking lot, just past the hairpin turn on NH 112.

The Wilderness Trail has probably become the most popular ski tour for newcomers to the White Mountains. Its name, some people complain, is a misnomer. But as with most popular destinations in the mountains, it attracts people for good reason.

The Wilderness Trail and the trails feeding into it are the gateway to the Pemigewasset Wilderness. This trail was the

Classic diagonal skiing on the Wilderness Trail alongside the
East Branch of the Pemigewasset River.

main line of the logging railroads a century ago. The old railroad ties still constitute the foundation of this heavily trekked thoroughfare. The trails in the area of the East Branch of the Pemigewasset River and around Mount Hitchcock are generally wide and well graded, as they had to be to accommodate the many trains that plied the routes. The setting of the Wilderness Trail makes for a classic cross-country ski tour as it travels alongside a wide river on nearly flat terrain. If your real joy in being on skis is just kicking and gliding for miles, this is the place to stretch out and cruise, while enjoying a beautiful backdrop.

A great day trip that will get you pumping is to ski the 13-mile loop around Mount Hitchcock. The route is best done east to west, since that maximizes the amount of downhill skiing. You will drop 1,600 feet in 4.7 miles on the Cedar Brook Trail on the way down to the Pemigewasset River.

From the start of the Hancock Notch Trail, the route passes through mixed forest on rolling terrain, running slightly uphill and traveling on wide, old railroad beds and logging roads. The junction with the Cedar Brook Trail is reached after 1.7 miles. The route continues on the Cedar Brook Trail, which can be tricky to follow at the beginning. The trail crosses the North Fork of the Hancock Branch five times within the first 0.6 mile. The first few crossings can be avoided by staying on the east side of the brook and following a rough trail. The Hancock Loop Trail to the summit of 4,403-foot Mount Hancock heads off east about 150 yards after the last crossing. Keep your eye out for the blue blazes throughout this section—if you lose sight of them, you are off the route and should backtrack.

After the junction with the Hancock Loop Trail, the Cedar Brook Trail climbs about 400 feet in the next 0.7 mile to the height-of-land between Mounts Hancock and Hitchcock. This is a beautiful boggy plateau with lodgepole tree trunks jutting toward the sky. The trail meanders along flat ground through a high meadow for a short distance before beginning the long, gradual descent down to the Pemigewasset River and the Wilderness Trail. The descent follows old logging roads that slab along the east side of the Cedar Brook drainage. The trail has a number of drainage divots that must be approached cautiously if there is light snow cover. You soon pass a sign that marks the old site of Camp 24A, one of J. H. Henry's logging outposts. This whole drainage was the site of intense logging activity by Henry's company at the turn of the century. The Cedar Brook Trail was originally the access route to five different logging camps, little evidence of which now remains.

The Cedar Brook Trail continues its steady descent until it drops down to the banks of the brook and makes a sharp right turn onto an old railroad bed at 4.1 miles. Soon after passing through the clearings of the old Camp 24, an unplowed access road (a rough grass road in the summer) which follows the east and south banks of the East Branch of the Pemigewasset River leaves to the left. This access road, which becomes FR 87 (unplowed), is a good alternate route back to the Kancamagus Highway (NH 112) which avoids the crowds that typically appear on the Wilderness Trail on weekends. It ends at the same parking lot as the Wilderness Trail. There is no sign marking its beginning on the Cedar Brook Trail, but it is an obvious major spur trail.

If you choose to continue to the Wilderness Trail, the Cedar Brook Trail heads down the old railroad beds at a slight downhill grade. It is just enough for arms-at-your-side gliding and watching the scenery as it opens up near the river. The views get more dramatic as the trail emerges from the deeper woods to vistas of the Bondcliffs and the farther reaches of the Pemigewasset Wilderness. This view is the essence of the Pemi: it is one the few regions in the Whites where you can experience being humbled by an uninterrupted stretch of wilderness. Gliding effortlessly into this untamed area will bring a smile to your face and a feeling that this is what backcountry skiing is all about.

The trip back on the Wilderness Trail is basically flat—6.3 miles of double-poling and aerobic diagonal stride skiing. This stretch can be very heavily traveled on weekends, as it attracts many novice cross-country skiers. The trail goes right alongside the East Branch of the Pemigewasset River, and the views are pleasant. From the parking lot, it is usually easy to get a ride back to your car at the start of the Hancock Notch Trail.

Pemigewasset Wilderness Region

Nancy and Norcross Ponds

THE TOUR   A ski tour to the isolated Nancy and Norcross ponds in the Pemigewasset Wilderness

LENGTH   Desolation Shelter to Nancy Pond: 4.6 miles; NH 302 to Nancy Pond: 3.5 miles; Nancy Pond to NH 302 via Carrigain Notch Trail and Sawyer River Road: 14.8 miles

ELEVATION   Starting (Desolation Shelter), 2,200 feet; Nancy Brook trailhead, 1,100 feet; high point: 3,100 feet

MAP   AMC map no. 5 (Franconia)

LEVEL OF DIFFICULTY   Moderate (from the west); more difficult (from the east)

HOW TO GET THERE   Desolation Shelter can be accessed from the south via the Carrigain Notch Trail or the Wilderness Trail. The Nancy Pond Trail begins on the west side of NH 302, 2.8 miles north of the Sawyer Rock picnic area and 6.7 miles south of the Willey House Site in Crawford Notch State Park.

Perched high on a plateau on the edge of the Pemigewasset Wilderness is a small network of four mountain ponds: Nancy, Norcross, Little Norcross, and Duck ponds. At 3,100 feet, they lie undisturbed and isolated, and offer sweeping views to the west of the entire Pemigewasset Wilderness. The actual

Looking west from Norcross Pond to the Franconia Ridge.

boundary of the designated Pemigewasset Wilderness Area cuts between Norcross and Nancy ponds. The U.S. Forest Service designated 460 acres around Nancy Pond as the Nancy Brook Scenic Area in 1964, to be maintained as much as possible in an undisturbed state. This action was taken partly to preserve a stand of virgin spruce on the north slopes of Duck Pond Mountain. This is said to be one of the two largest areas of virgin timber in the state.

The ponds are a perfect day trip destination for a party that is camping in the Pemi. Accessed from the west, the Nancy Pond Trail ascends an abandoned railroad bed that is a delightful mile-long gentle downhill run on the return. From Desolation Shelter, the Carrigain Notch Trail is followed for 1 mile until it intersects the Nancy Pond Trail, which continues straight ahead. The terrain is flat and straight, perfect for fast backcountry flat-tracking. The trail crosses a number of streams and brooks, some of which are bridged by single logs. Bold skiers can keep their skis on and test their balance on these, or one can choose a less airy alternative by either walking or skiing across a frozen section of the drainage nearby. The route then parallels Norcross Brook as it climbs gently (skins are not needed) up the drainage that leads to Norcross Pond. The ski tour begins in dense fir and hemlock forests, which give way to open birch stands with increasing elevation.

This ski tour offers access to a wild area. There is a wonderful sense of isolation at these ponds, windswept and eery in their desolation. Few people ski to the ponds from the west because it is not a feasible day trip from the road. But the rewards make it worth the effort of planning an overnight trip. Norcross Pond has one of the most spectacular views over the Pemigewasset valley, with views of the Franconia Ridge, Mounts Bond and Guyot, and even a glimpse into Zealand Notch. One also has a clear view here of three slides on Mount Nancy, which look as if they would be good ski descents; logging roads can be followed on Mount Nancy to get to them.

As you travel east, Nancy Pond lies another mile down the

trail. You can practice a little backcountry skating technique as you cross the snowy, wind-scoured ponds.

The ascent to the ponds from the east is a little more difficult. The route follows old logging roads for the first 2 miles, then crosses some old landslides and a drainage. At 2.4 miles the trail reaches the Nancy Cascades, a beautiful, ledgy falls. The trail skirts the falls on the left via steep switchbacks through the woods. It is easiest to remove skis and walk this section. The trail then covers easy ground through a virgin spruce forest, emerging at Nancy Pond in 3.5 miles.

To make a loop through Carrigain Notch and return to NH 302, the Carrigain Notch Trail leaves the Nancy Pond Trail 2.8 miles west of Norcross Pond at a well-marked junction. The trail climbs moderately on an old logging road, reaching Carrigain Notch (elevation 2,639 feet) in 1.8 miles. The trail follows logging roads down from the notch, and several steep downhill chutes must be negotiated. Easier ground is reached, and an area of beaver activity is crossed. The Signal Ridge Trail junction is reached 2.3 miles after the notch. Follow the Signal Ridge Trail over fairly flat ground for 1.7 miles until it ends at the Sawyer River Road. The Sawyer River Road is unplowed all the way to NH 302. It is heavily used by snowmobiles, making it a fast 2-mile ski to NH 302.

Carter Dome

THE TOUR   The Carter Dome Trail and the Nineteen-Mile Brook Trail provide access to Carter Dome and Carter Notch, a striking cleft with towering rock walls that is home to an AMC hut. The classic descent is via the Carter Dome Trail.

LENGTH   10 miles round-trip to Carter Dome summit (either via Carter Notch or climbing and descending the Carter Dome Trail to the summit)

ELEVATION   Starting: 1,500 feet; high point: 4,832 feet

MAPS   AMC map no. 7 (Carter-Mahoosuc) or AMC map no. 6 (Mount Washington Range)

DIFFICULTY   Most difficult

HOW TO GET THERE   The trailhead for the Nineteen-Mile Brook Trail is 1 mile north of the Mount Washington Auto Road on NH 16.

The Carter Notch area has long been underused by skiers. The ignorance of skiers has been the bliss of snowshoers, as evidenced by the fact that the AMC Carter Notch Hut is packed with the latter every weekend. As a result, there is much ski exploration that has yet to be done in this area. As one of two areas served by an AMC hut that is open in the winter (the Zealand valley is the other), the possibilities for multiday ski tours and day trips from the hut are plentiful.

Carrying skis is the easiest way to negotiate the steep trail from Carter Notch to the summit of Carter Dome.

The tours in this area are of a more rugged nature than those accessed from the AMC Zealand Falls Hut, but more advanced skiers looking for challenging runs will be rewarded in a variety of ways for the trip into this relatively untamed region.

The 5-mile-long mountain ridge that begins with Shelburne Moriah Mountain in the north and ends with the E peak of Wildcat Mountain has always gotten short shrift from visitors to the area, since it lies in the proverbial shadow of its majestic cousins in the Presidential Range to the west. White Mountain travelers might be surprised, therefore, to learn that six summits on this ridge are over 4,000 feet high, and that some of the most spectacular scenery in the White Mountains can be found here.

The most striking feature of this long ridge is Carter Notch. Glaciers deepened what was already a passageway that separated the Wildcat Ridge in the southwest from the Carter-Moriah Ridge to the northeast. Carter Notch was the result, a vertical drop of 1,600 feet from the summit of Carter Dome and 1,200 feet from Wildcat Mountain. Towering cliffs, two glacial tarns, and numerous giant boulders and blocks lying strewn helter-skelter about the notch floor are the impressive detritus of mountain formation.

The shortest route into the notch is via the Nineteen Mile Brook Trail, which is a 3.8-mile ski from NH 16 to the Carter Notch Hut. This trail is heavily traveled by snowshoers and hikers, so expect hard-packed snow. The trail climbs gently alongside the Nineteen-Mile Brook, a beautiful and picturesque drainage that is fed by springs and runoff from Carter Dome and Wildcat. A few sections of the trail become obstructed by ice flows from above; these sections may be skirted by descending to the brook and skiing carefully around them.

The junction with the Carter Dome Trail is reached after 1.9 miles. The Nineteen Mile Brook Trail to the notch gets progressively steeper from here. The notch and Wildcat Mountain come into view at a birch glade about a half mile up from the trail junction. In the final quarter mile before the

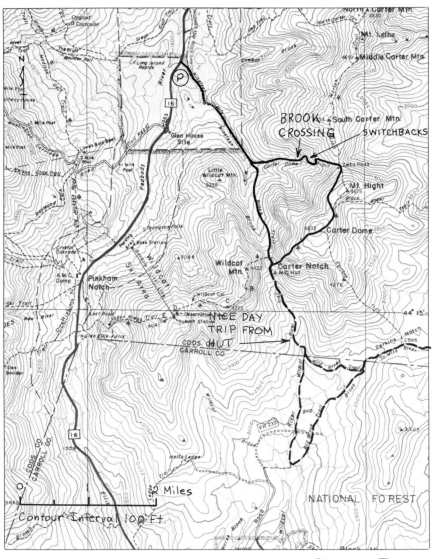

Carter Dome

notch, the trail pitches up very steeply and has several switch-backs. Even people as familiar with the trail as the hut keep-ers chuckle about and warn skiers of what a hair-raising de-scent this last section can be.

Built in 1904, the stone-constructed Carter Notch Hut is the oldest hut still in active use by the AMC. It has two separate bunkhouses that sleep a total of forty. The hut keep-ers are good sources of information about trail conditions and recent precipitation. Check with them if you are in doubt as to your choice of descent routes.

There are a number of options for the descent. The classic ski tour would include the exciting Carter Dome Trail. If you are doing a day trip from NH 16, you may want to access the Carter Dome Trail from its junction with the Nineteen-Mile Brook Trail. It is 3.1 miles from this junction to the summit of Carter Dome. From Carter Notch, the mile-long climb to the summit of Carter Dome on the Carter-Moriah Trail is ex-tremely steep at the beginning and is best negotiated by car-rying your skis and kicking steps up it. If you happen to be skiing this loop in reverse, you would be well advised to de-scend this latter section in the same fashion. Throughout the climb you are treated to more and more impressive views down into the notch and across to the cliffs flanking Wildcat.

The summit of Carter Dome is covered with low scrub and offers excellent views. The Carter Dome Trail begins here, coinciding with the Carter-Moriah Trail for the next 1.1 miles, except where the two trails diverge briefly around Mount Hight. This section of the trail travels along a wild mountain ridge. It adds an exciting alpine element to the ski tour and is part of what makes this such a classic. If you are ascending the Carter Dome Trail, the climb to the Carter Dome summit from Zeta Pass is well worth the extra effort.

The summit of Mount Hight offers some of the best views along the ridge but is rocky and is usually not skiable. The Carter Dome Trail skirts this rocky peak to the west and is the recommended ski route. The trail follows a tricky sidehill as it slabs down the side of the ridge, making it awkward to ski for about a half mile.

The descent from Zeta Pass to the Nineteen-Mile Brook Trail offers the best skiing on this tour. The trail follows an abandoned road that used to serve a long-dismantled fire tower on the summit of Carter Dome. The upper section, from Zeta Pass to a tributary that feeds the Nineteen-Mile Brook, is only 8–10 feet wide and drops relatively steeply. Seven sharp switchback turns on this upper section will keep you on your toes. The trail is lightly traveled and usually accumulates a good deal of powder.

Once the trail crosses to the south side of the tributary, the switchbacks end and the grade becomes much more moderate and considerably wider. This makes for delightful moderate telemarking all the way to the junction with the Nineteen-Mile Brook Trail. For those wanting a shorter day trip with some enjoyable downhill skiing, a round-trip from the trailhead to this brook crossing on the Carter Dome Trail would be a good choice.

Good judgment must be used in deciding whether to go to the summit of Carter Dome on this tour. The Carter-Moriah Ridge, which the trail follows as it drops to Zeta Pass, is exposed to the full force of the elements. If the weather is dubious, skiing to the summit should probably be abandoned. The route down is difficult, and conditions on it can vary considerably, depending to some extent on whether it has been rutted out by snowshoers. Even in good conditions, this ski tour requires a party of strong skiers.

Other Options. Descending the Nineteen-Mile Brook Trail requires fast reflexes in the upper sections, but it is an enjoyable moderate descent after the Carter Dome Trail junction. The trail usually has a narrow snowshoe trough and resulting icy sections. When descending this trail, *be careful of hikers*. You are likely to meet people on this trail even midweek.

A nice day trip from the hut is to take the Wildcat River Trail south from the notch. The first half mile is quite steep and usually walked, but the skiing after this is open and moderate to the Wild River Trail, which leads to the Bog Brook Trail. From the Bog Brook–Wild River trail junction, a beautiful route goes west through Perkins Notch to No-Ketchum Pond. You may then backtrack to the Wildcat River Trail and climb back to the hut.

A few tips on trails *not* to ski: both the Rainbow Trail and the Black Angel Trail, which leave to the southeast and east, respectively, from the summit of Carter Dome, are narrow, overgrown, and steep at the top. The best skiing on these trails is the open glades on their lower sections, which can be accessed from the Wild River Trail.

Wildcat Valley Trail

THE TOUR   A ski tour from Wildcat Mountain to the town of Jackson, New Hampshire

LENGTH   11 miles

ELEVATION   Starting (Wildcat gondola upper station): 4,000 feet; ending: 755 feet

MAPS   AMC map no. 7 (Carter-Mahoosuc); AMC map no. 6 (Mount Washington Range); the AMC *Mount Washington and the Heart of the Presidential Range* map (shows the first third of the route) and the *Jackson Ski Touring Map,* available at the Jack Frost Ski Shop in Jackson or at the AMC Pinkham Notch Camp, are the only maps that show this trail

DIFFICULTY   More difficult

FEE   This is a fee trail of the Jackson Ski Touring Foundation (603-383-9355). A reduced-fee ticket for skiing only the Wildcat Valley Trail must be purchased at the Jackson Ski Touring Foundation office in Jackson (located in the Jack Frost Ski Shop). Showing your JSTF trail ticket also entitles you to a reduced rate on the gondola.

HOW TO GET THERE   From Jackson, drive north on NH 16 to the Wildcat Ski Area. Purchase single-ride gondola tickets. The trail begins behind the upper gondola station. An AMC skier shuttle van is available in the afternoon from the Dana Place Inn or Jackson back to the Wildcat Ski Area.

Dana Pl. Trail: ; easy from Dana Pl. up aways, and then down at the st. ?

Descending the upper section of the Wildcat Valley Trail.
Photograph by Roger Leo.

The Wildcat Valley Trail has become perhaps the most popular down-mountain backcountry ski trail in New England today. Cut in 1972 by volunteers for the Jackson Ski Touring Foundation, the run was meant to be the adrenaline-pumping jewel in the network of trails that link the town of Jackson with the surrounding White Mountains. Over a decade and a half later, the goal of the original trail crews is still achieved every time an unsuspecting skier drops down off the summit of Wildcat Mountain to begin the 3,245-foot descent into Jackson.

The Wildcat Valley Trail offers a unique New England skiing experience. The ski tour travels the full range of the local mountain environment in its 11 miles. Beginning near treeline between the windswept "D" and "E" peaks of Wildcat Mountain, the trail quickly drops into thick spruce groves, so familiar in the White Mountains. Over the course of the afternoon it takes to ski the trail, skiers will pass through old farm pastures, traverse across stands of mountain birch, and follow abandoned logging roads. Although it does not qualify as a pure wilderness tour, it makes up for what it reveals of human transgressions by providing a glimpse of past decades of New England culture.

This trail has a formidable ancestry to uphold. One of the most popular of the CCC's down-mountain ski trails from the 1930s was the Wildcat Trail, a Class A race trail on the northwest side of Wildcat Mountain. It boasted a vertical drop of 2,000 feet in a mile and a half, with grades as steep as 33 degrees. The old Wildcat Trail eventually formed the hub of the trail network of the Wildcat Ski Area, and substantially the same route can still be skied today with chairlift access. Since the loss of the Wildcat Trail to the downhill ski area, it took some thirty years for Wildcat Mountain to become home again to a trail for backcountry skiers looking for challenging down-mountain skiing.

Just because backcountry skiers lost a treasured ski trail to a lift-served ski area doesn't mean they have to reject the conveniences that it now provides. The easiest and quickest access to the Wildcat Valley Trail is gained by purchasing a

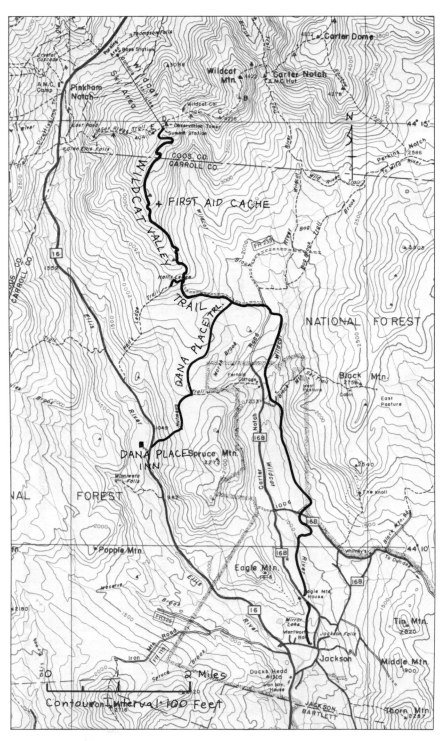

Wildcat Valley Trail

single-ride gondola ticket to the top of the mountain. If you feel pangs of guilt about this, you can ski up the mountain, as long as you stay out of the way of oncoming skiers.

The trail begins just behind (south of) the summit cafeteria and upper gondola station. A weathered sign marking the start of the route warns skiers about the difficult nature of the trail. Heed these words if they apply to you: despite the popularity of this route, it is still a committing undertaking that is not suitable for beginning skiers. Rescue is difficult, and the skiing can be fast and treacherous in icy or crusty conditions.

The trail starts inauspiciously: the first 50 feet are typically plastered with windblown ice. The trail then switches back with a few quick blind corners and downhill runs that alternate with flatter terrain. The numerous sitzmarks testify to the technique many people revert to on this section. The trail passes through birch glades, and drops steadily until it reaches Hall's Ledge after 3.2 miles. Hall's Ledge is a traditional lunch stop on the route, and it offers dramatic views across the valley into the Gulf of Slides, Tuckerman Ravine, and Huntington Ravine on Mount Washington.

From Hall's Ledge, the trail follows a logging road and takes a mile-long straight, fast drop into the Prospect Farm area. At this point, two-thirds of the vertical drop on this route has been skied. Just down the trail from here, a junction with the Dana Place Trail is reached. From here, the alternatives are to turn right and continue 4.4 miles to the Dana Place Inn via the Dana Place Trail and the Hutsmen Trail, or to continue straight on the Wildcat Valley Trail 6.8 miles to Jackson.

The Dana Place Trail follows an old logging road on easy rolling terrain, turning right where it intersects the Marsh Brook Trail after 0.9 mile. After passing through an abandoned apple orchard, the trail then joins with the Hutsmen Trail, dropping down more quickly until it reaches a plowed parking pullout across the road from the Dana Place Inn.

If you elect to continue on the Wildcat Valley Trail into Jackson, the trail continues straight ahead from the Dana Place Trail junction, eventually crossing open fields and hitting the Carter Notch Road. Skiers must walk on the road for 0.5 mile to Black Mountain Terrace, where they must turn left and pass the town dump (!) before the trail resumes on the right. Be alert for blue plastic blazes as you continue. After 2.2 miles, the trail crosses NH 16B, continues through an old logging area and some fields, and crosses two bridges and the Eagle Mountain Golf Course before again crossing NH 16B 1.7 miles after first crossing it. The trail picks up on the other side of the road and continues for 0.5 mile before ending at the Wentworth Resort in Jackson. At this point you will probably be ready to take advantage of this trail's greatest feature: the opportunity to end the route right at one of Jackson's several drinking establishments.

Ski conditions on this route vary considerably. The trail will often have a new dusting of snow up high, even when conditions look dubious in the valley. However, if it has rained recently or there is an icy crust, the skiing is treacherous at best. The Jackson Ski Touring Foundation can provide information on current trail conditions.

The main drawback to this ski tour is the price: after paying for a trail pass and a single-ride gondola ticket, this can be an expensive day of play. Recognizing this, the Jackson Ski Touring Foundation instituted a reduced-fee trail ticket for skiing the Wildcat Valley Trail beginning in 1988. Skiers should be advised that courtesy patrollers on this and other JSTF trails will charge an extra fee to people who have not purchased a ticket beforehand, and that the reduced-fee ticket does not permit skiing on the other JSTF trails (you may upgrade your ticket in Jackson if you decide you want to continue skiing on other trails).

Mount Washington Region

Mount Washington (elevation 6,288 feet) is the crown of the White Mountains. It is also the highest point in the Northeast and the third highest mountain in the East. Standing watch over New England, Mount Washington has always been a magnet for winter explorers. Ice climbers, snowshoers, cross-country skiers, and alpine skiers all share the trails on this mountain as they make their way to their respective meccas. Much of the history of skiing in this region is presented in the section on Tuckerman Ravine.

The skiing in the Mount Washington region is distinctive for its alpine character. All of the ski tours described in this section are set in the heart of the White Mountains, offering sweeping views of surrounding peaks and valleys. Some of the routes, such as Tuckerman Ravine and the Gulf of Slides, are unique for New England. They offer wide, open bowl skiing above timberline, much like skiing in the larger mountain ranges of the western United States.

There are vast wilderness skiing opportunities in this region (see the Gulf of Slides route description for other suggestions). Skiing the classic routes described in this section will, it is hoped, inspire skiers to strike out in search of other, more remote, but equally rewarding ski tours.

A Note on Maps. The best map of the Mount Washington region is the AMC's *Mount Washington and the Heart of the Presidential Range* (1988), by Bradford Washburn. It is a beautiful and painstakingly precise map by the man who drew the definitive maps of Mount McKinley and Mount Everest. It covers all of the routes described in this section. Also useful are

AMC map no. 6 (Mount Washington Range) and the *Jackson Ski Touring Map*. These maps are available at the AMC Pinkham Notch Camp and at the Jack Frost Ski Shop in Jackson.

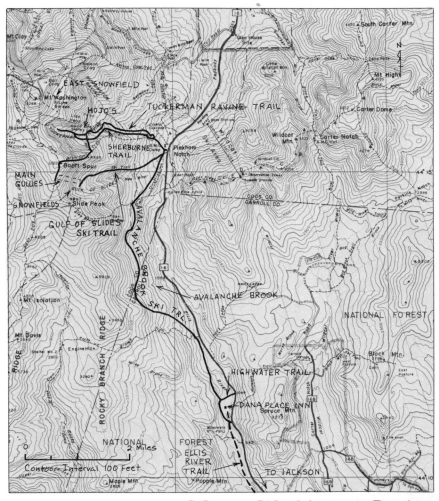

Mount Washington Region

Tuckerman Ravine

Sherburne Trail

Gulf of Slides

Avalanche Brook

Mount Washington Region

Avalanche Brook Trail

THE TOUR   A rugged ski trail with good downhill runs from Pinkham Notch to the Dana Place Inn in Jackson

LENGTH   5.5 miles

ELEVATION   Starting: 2,000 feet; high point: 2,650 feet; ending: 1,000 feet

MAPS   AMC map no. 6 (Mount Washington Range) covers this terrain, but the trail is not shown. The AMC *Mount Washington and the Heart of the Presidential Range* map (shows all but the last mile) and the *Jackson Ski Touring Map* are the only ones that show this trail.

DIFFICULTY   More difficult

HOW TO GET THERE   The trail begins at the south end of the parking lot at the AMC Pinkham Notch Camp off NH 16.

T he Avalanche Brook Trail is an exciting run that passes through mixed forest in the heart of the White Mountains. It goes south from Pinkham Notch Camp, the northern center of operations for the Appalachian Mountain Club, to the Dana Place Inn in Jackson.

The Avalanche Brook Trail was cut by volunteers of the Appalachian Mountain Club in 1975. It was designed to link

Crossing an open stream drainage on the Avalanche Brook Trail. Photograph by Roger Leo.

the growing trail network in the town of Jackson with the AMC's ski trail network in the Pinkham Notch area. The original plan was to cut a trail down the east side of NH 16, where the terrain is relatively gentle. When the trail designers could not figure out a way to skirt the precipitous and rocky drop-off around Glen Ellis Falls, they turned their attention to the west side of the valley. The views from the west side were considered superior, but the trail builders had to level out a bothersome sidehill in several places. The final result was the Avalanche Brook Trail. Once the trail was completed, it became possible to traverse the entire length of Pinkham Notch, beginning on trails from the Glen House (across from the Mount Washington Auto Road) and skiing all the way to Jackson. The trail now enjoys steady traffic throughout the winter.

This tour, while not a high mountain experience, travels through interesting mixed forests with a nice variety of terrain. It offers an enjoyable half day of skiing. When it begins its descent, there is not much time for dallying. It heads fairly fast for the valley floor, dropping more than 1,500 feet in 2.5 miles. The trail runs parallel to NH 16, and is well marked. The route is almost always skied from north to south, since the longest downhill sections run in this direction. The AMC skier shuttle bus is available, for a fee, to transport skiers from either end of the trail back to their cars.

The trail begins at the south end of the parking lot at the Pinkham Notch Camp. A sign at the trailhead informs you that the route follows the Gulf of Slides Ski Trail for the first 0.2 mile. Go straight ahead, cross a wooden bridge over the New River, and watch for a sign pointing left that directs you to the Avalanche Brook Trail.

From Pinkham Notch, there are beautiful views into Huntington Ravine to the northwest, while the craggy summit of Boott Spur lies due west. The Gulf of Slides Ski Trail diverges to the right after 0.2 mile; the Avalanche Brook Trail continues to the left following blue blazes. The trail meanders through hardwood forests on flat ground. The Glen Boulder

Trail intersects the trail at 1.7 miles, after which the Avalanche Brook Trail climbs steeply for a short stretch, then levels out and contours along the side of Slide Peak. The Glen Boulder can be seen above to the west. The trail crosses the lower end of an old avalanche path, the result of a 1967 mud slide from the Glen Boulder ridge above. The trail continues through mixed forest, with beautiful views of the Carter Range across the valley. Rounding the side of a broad ridge that runs from Slide Peak, the trail descends briefly and then contours at 2,300 feet for another mile. After a gradual climb, the trail crosses a wooden bridge over Avalanche Brook, a deep, ravine-like drainage. From this point, the trail plunges downhill for the next 2 miles.

Good trail work has been done on this route, with wooden bridges now spanning most of the deeper drainages. AMC trail crews replaced all the bridges on the trail in 1988.

This relatively narrow trail does not allow much room for graceful swooping turns; a better approach would be to "stay low and go." This is not a ski tour on which to be hesitant and tense. The tour is most fun when you are in the mood to ski aggressively and don't mind seeing the birches go by fast. It is, however, a forgiving route: there is ample room to bail out almost anywhere you choose.

After about 5 miles and a fast descent, the trail crosses the Hall Trail (an unplowed road). If you miss this cutoff and come out at the Rocky Branch trailhead, you may continue for a few minutes along the right side of a parking lot and join the Hall Trail behind a metal gate on the south end of the lot. Blue blazes continue to mark the way. Within 0.25 mile of the gate, a sign pointing left directs you to the final section of the Avalanche Brook Trail, which intersects with the highwater trail behind the Dana Place Inn. From this junction you may turn left, and you will emerge on NH 16 just north of the Dana Place Inn. If you choose to turn right at this junction, the trail soon intersects with the Ellis River Trail, which proceeds another 4.7 miles south on flat ground to the town of Jackson (if you choose to continue to Jackson, you will be on a fee trail of the Jackson Ski Touring Foundation trail system; trail tickets may be purchased at the Dana Place Inn). Turning left on the Ellis River Trail brings you to the Dana Place Inn in several minutes.

Finishing up at the Dana Place Inn, you will find clear views to the north across the fields to the snowy summit of Mount Washington and the peaks running south of it.

Mount Washington Region
Gulf of Slides

THE TOUR   The Gulf of Slides Ski Trail drops down from the base of the ravine from which the trail gets its name. There is excellent steep skiing in the Gulf of Slides itself and good downhill skiing on the trail.

LENGTH   Gulf of Slides Ski Trail: 2.5 miles

ELEVATION   Starting: 2,000 feet; ski trail high point: 3,900 feet; Gulf headwall high point: 5,000 feet

MAPS   AMC map no. 6 (Mount Washington Range); AMC *Mount Washington and the Heart of the Presidential Range* map

DIFFICULTY   Most difficult

HOW TO GET THERE   The Gulf of Slides Ski Trail leaves from the south end of the parking lot at the AMC Pinkham Notch Camp.

The Gulf of Slides has long been neglected by the majority of skiers. It is well away from the crowds that flock to the bowl in Tuckerman Ravine—indeed, it is unknown to many of the Tuck's regulars. That is precisely its appeal.

The Gulf of Slides is a wide ravine between ridges that run off of Boott Spur (elevation 5,500 feet) and Slide Peak (elevation 4,806 feet). The slides for which it is named form along

Catching air in one of the main gullies on the headwall of the Gulf of Slides.

the east-facing headwall and can be seen from the highway below. The Gulf of Slides holds some of the latest snow in the White Mountains outside of Tuckerman Ravine. It is a traditional spring skiing destination, with ski activity usually continuing from mid-March through May.

Skiing in the Gulf of Slides has historically been reserved for the smaller number of skiers interested in exploring other slopes in the Mount Washington area. Although skiers began venturing into Tuckerman Ravine in the late 1920s, it wasn't until the early 1930s that those same skiers made their way into the Gulf of Slides. That they finally came was inevitable; the long snowfields of the Gulf are visible from a number of vantage points in the Mount Washington valley and hold obvious promise for skiing. Al Sise, one of the first of the Tuckerman skiers, recalls that the Gulf of Slides was simply "where someone would go to get away from the crowds. . . . It was not as awe-inspiring a place [as Tuckerman Ravine], but it was a nice place to get away from it all and ski."

The first skiers in the Gulf of Slides bushwhacked their way up the New River from the AMC Pinkham Notch Camp to reach the headwall. By all accounts, it was not a leisurely trip. Some skiers accessed it from the top by climbing up to the Davis Path, returning to Pinkham Notch by skiing the snow-filled bed of the New River ("a tough go," recalls one of those skiers). Interest and activity in the Gulf picked up enough in the early thirties to warrant a bona fide trail. In 1935 Charlie Proctor designed and laid out the Gulf of Slides Ski Trail from Pinkham Notch, following the north bank of the New River into the Gulf. The trail was cut that same year by the CCC, and it has been maintained as a ski trail ever since. A few races were held on the trail, but because of the lack of any shelters in the Gulf of Slides area, it was considered a less hospitable place for races than other, more developed trails in the valley. Unlike the Sherburne Trail, which has been widened and rerouted in places, the Gulf of Slides Ski Trail has not been significantly changed from its original state.

Lacking the crowds, the Gulf of Slides has not enjoyed the kind of ski lore of Tuckerman Ravine, where every ski run has a name and a reputation. The more popular runs on the Gulf of Slides headwall were given rather uninteresting names, although few skiers today even know the runs have names. Brooks Dodge, son of the legendary AMC huts manager Joe Dodge and an early skier in the Gulf, says they were identified from north to south as the Boott Spur gully, the main gullies, the left gully, and the snowfield, which is the large slope that runs north from Slide Peak. The names are less important than the fact that virtually all the gullies and snowfields on the headwall of the Gulf of Slides that start from Boott Spur have been skied and are skiable.

The lower end of the Gulf of Slides Ski Trail lies at the south end of the parking lot at the AMC Pinkham Notch Camp and branches off from the bottom of the Sherburne Trail. Beginning from the parking lot, the start of the trail is the same as that of the Avalanche Brook Trail; the trails diverge after 0.2 mile, where the Gulf of Slides Ski Trail heads right. The trail is about 20 feet wide and climbs steadily; the steepest grade is about 20 degrees. There are nice views to the east of the Carter-Moriah Ridge and the Wildcat Ridge as the trail climbs. There is a rescue cache with a litter just before the trail crosses the New River near the top of the trail. There are no views of the slides themselves until this point.

The Gulf of Slides Ski Trail is an enjoyable run in itself. Skied from the top, it is a sustained, 2.5-mile downhill run similar in character to the Sherburne Trail, but not as steep as the lower sections of the Sherburne. If avalanche conditions exist on the slides (see note at the end of this section), just skiing the trail is a day well spent.

The upper end of the ski trail lies at the foot of the most prominent slide, which is just left of center on the headwall. This slide is about half a mile long, running all the way to the ridge at the top of the headwall. There is another shorter and slightly narrower slide to the right of it. Both of these slides get progressively steeper as they rise. Skiers can climb up as high as they are comfortable and ski down them. From where the Gulf of Slides Ski Trail ends, one can also continue bushwhacking south through widely spaced spruce trees and enter the base of a very large snowfield that runs north from Slide Peak. This snowfield is not visible from the main gullies. The snowfield slopes are more moderate.

The gullies on the far right running down from Boott Spur are most easily accessed by climbing the steep Boott Spur Link Trail, which leaves south from the Tuckerman Ravine Trail just opposite the foot of the Lion Head Trail. The slides at the center of the headwall can also be accessed by dropping down from Boott Spur in this way, although it is 0.8 mile longer than the approach on the Gulf of Slides Ski Trail. From Pinkham Notch Camp it is 3.6 miles to the summit of Boott Spur via the Boott Spur Link Trail and another 0.2 mile south on the Davis Path to the top of the main slide.

The Gulf of Slides is an extraordinary skiing area. A first reaction on seeing the slides and the snowfield is one of amazement that such terrain can be found in New England. Wide, open bowl skiing and steep alpine runs look like the Colorado backcountry. Climbing high up on the slides one has panoramic views up and down the valley. There is a wild, untamed feeling about the place.

A trip into the Gulf of Slides is a good way to inspire skiers about the other possibilities for wilderness skiing in the White Mountains. The Gulf is one of a number of outlying ravines that are rarely visited by skiers. Oakes Gulf, Ammonoosuc Ravine, King Ravine, Jefferson Ravine, and the Mount Jefferson snowfields are just some of the many excellent skiing jewels that skiers with a lust for exploration have had to themselves. If you are at all enchanted by the idea of laying first tracks or stumbling upon a snowfield or gully that may never have been skied, you need only pick up your map and head out. There is skiing everywhere, and the opportunities for exploring new terrain are limitless.

A word of caution to skiers: the Gulf of Slides is so named because it is highly prone to avalanches. Early in the winter, before the snowpack has consolidated, is the most unstable time. The gullies in the Gulf tend to avalanche more frequently than those in Tuckerman Ravine because the slopes in the Gulf are more uniform and the ground below the snow is smoother. Check the signboard in the AMC Pinkham Notch Camp, which lists avalanche conditions, for some guidance, but the final assessment must be made by each skier. The Gulf of Slides is not the place to go just after a large snowfall, when its 30–40-degree slopes are most likely to slide. This is a remote area, and help will be a long time in coming in the event of an accident. Prevention, such as avoiding slopes whose stability you are unsure of, is essential.

John Sherburne Ski Trail

THE TOUR   A 2.4-mile downhill run from just above the Hermit Lake shelters to the AMC Pinkham Notch Camp

LENGTH   4.8 miles round-trip from Pinkham Notch Camp

ELEVATION   Starting: 4,000 feet; ending: 2,000 feet

MAPS   AMC map no. 6 (Mount Washington Range); AMC *Mount Washington and the Heart of the Presidential Range* map

DIFFICULTY   More difficult

HOW TO GET THERE   From Pinkham Notch Camp on NH 16, take the Tuckerman Ravine Trail 2.4 miles uphill to the Hermit Lake shelters. The spur to the Sherburne Trail is directly opposite the porch at the Hermit Lake shelters caretaker's building (Ho-Jo's).

The John Sherburne Ski Trail is viewed by most alpine skiers simply as the end-of-the-day run home after a day of skiing in Tuckerman Ravine. But for Nordic skiers, it deserves much more attention than just a footnote to an afternoon in the bowl. It is an enjoyable downhill ski run and a worthwhile destination in its own right.

Coming down the Sherburne Trail, with Mount Washington in the background.

The Sherburne Trail was designed and laid out by Charles Proctor and cut in 1934. It was named for John H. Sherburne, Jr., a well-liked ski racer and member of the Ski Club Hochgebirge of Boston who was instrumental in starting the famous American Inferno races in Tuckerman Ravine. He died unexpectedly of tetanus in 1934.

The need for a descending ski trail from Tuckerman Ravine was becoming more critical as the popularity of skiing in the bowl increased. Before the Sherburne Trail was built, the ravine was served only by the old Fire Trail, now known as the Tuckerman Ravine Trail. Skiing was always prohibited on the Fire Trail since it posed a serious threat to unsuspecting hikers ambling up the trail. But walking downhill for nearly 3 miles with skis over one's shoulder didn't sit right with Tuckerman Ravine regulars, and everyone agreed that another alternative had to be found. The solution was and continues to be the John Sherburne Ski Trail. The traffic rules that were established in the 1930s still hold today: skiing downhill is strictly forbidden on the Tuckerman Ravine Trail, and the Sherburne is reserved solely for downhill skiing (that is, no snowshoeing or hiking is permitted).

The Sherburne is a wide trail, cut with skiers in mind. There is ample room to choose your own line and ski it as you like. It is also the route that the rangers drive from Hermit Lake down to Pinkham Notch in their snow machines. This has a mixed effect: the snow machines pack the trail, keeping snow on it for a longer period of time, but it is common to encounter choppy tracks that make skiing difficult. Fortunately, the Sherburne Trail is often replenished with a new layer of snow to cover old tracks since it catches a good dose of the frequent snowstorms on Mount Washington.

The route begins innocently enough, 0.2 mile above HoJo's on flat terrain at the base of the Little Headwall. Early in the season it is possible to ski all the way from Tuckerman Ravine to Pinkham Notch via the Little Headwall. Spring skiers may never know of the existence of the Little Headwall, since it has usually turned into a waterfall by late April. The Sherburne soon passes just south of HoJo's, separated from it by a wooden bridge over the Cutler River. Most skiers who have just come to ski the Sherburne begin their descent at this bridge. The trail drops gently at the start. The views across the valley to the Wildcat Ridge and Carter Dome are worth stopping to admire. There are also impressive views into both Tuckerman and Huntington ravines to the west and northwest.

As with many trails of its era, the memorable moments on the Sherburne were all given names by the early skiers. The trail runs parallel to the south fork of the Cutler River but turns sharply southeast away from the drainage 0.6 mile below HoJo's. This turn was known as Windy Corner, and it was once the site of a cabin, since removed, built by the Harvard Mountaineering Club. Windy Corner got its name because it was always blasted by winds from the ravine and was consequently icy and windblown. The U.S. Forest Service recently relocated the section of the trail at Windy Corner so it would be less exposed to the weather.

The Sherburne gets progressively steeper as it descends. At 1.6 miles down the trail, the S-Turn is reached, so named because the trail swings back and forth in the shape of the letter S. From here down was considered one of the most difficult points of the Sherburne when races were held on it. Just below the S-Turn is the Schuss, a sharp left-hand turn with a steep, straight drop. The trail then passes through the Bottleneck, a sharp, narrow right-hand turn, then into the Glade, an open, moderately steep slope. The final steep drop is Deadman's Curve, where the trail drops steeply and turns sharply to the right. This last section received its name because a skier hit a tree here and was killed in the 1930s. The tree was promptly removed.

The steepest sections (up to 24 degrees) are encountered in the last third of the route. The trail is as much as 60 feet wide at this final section, though, so you are still left with many options as to how to negotiate the crux moves.

The Sherburne Trail can be deceptive. Over 2 miles of linking turns is no small job at the end of a day. This run can be a delight if you have the energy for it, and an endurance test if you've blown your strength having too much fun else-where that day. It has certainly caught me off guard. I have skied this trail smiling all the way one day and whining for my partners to wait up the next.

The Sherburne Trail is an excellent introduction to down-mountain skiing for people who have gotten the hang of some cross-country downhill techniques on lift-served ski slopes and want to try them out in the mountains. The trail is wide enough to take long traversing turns, will certainly introduce you to some unpredictable snow conditions, and will call for some creative thinking in your approach to some of the obsta-cles. In addition, it has the unusual distinction of beginning just below one of the meccas of mountain skiing, Tuckerman Ravine. If you are a newcomer to this sport, a side trip into the bowl to see what you can aspire to ski should give you new incentive to keep practicing those turns. The exciting stuff will be waiting for you just around the corner.

Mount Washington Region
Tuckerman Ravine

THE TOURS   A variety of extremely steep and challenging ski routes in the area in and near Tuckerman Ravine on Mount Washington

LENGTH   From Pinkham Notch to Hermit Lake shelters: 2.4 miles; to floor of Tuckerman Ravine: 3.1 miles

ELEVATION   Pinkham Notch: 2,000 feet; Tuckerman Ravine floor: 4,400 feet; Mount Washington summit: 6,288 feet

MAPS   AMC map no. 6 (Mount Washington Range); AMC *Mount Washington and the Heart of the Presidential Range* map

DIFFICULTY   Most difficult

HOW TO GET THERE   Tuckerman Ravine is reached via the Tuckerman Ravine Trail, which leaves behind the AMC Pinkham Notch Camp.

If skiers from west of the Mississippi River have heard of no other mountain ski routes in the East, they have probably still heard of Tuckerman Ravine.

Tuckerman Ravine—referred to affectionately as "Tuck's," or simply "the bowl"—is where skiing legends have been made, broken, and made up. It is the home of some of the

Descending the center of the headwall in Tuckerman Ravine, with spectators watching from Lunch Rocks.

steepest established backcountry ski runs in the country and usually holds the last snows of the year, when every other place in New England has long since turned to rock and dirt. It is viewed by skiers alternately as a proving ground and a playground, depending on their abilities.

The ravine is a huge glacial cirque. It is named for botanist Edward Tuckerman, who explored the White Mountains for two decades in the mid-1800s. Most of the snow that collects in the bowl is deposited by wind, which is generally out of the west-northwest and carries snow from the Bigelow Lawn and the summit cone of the mountain. Snow on the floor of the bowl may reach depths of 75–100 feet.

A Brief History of Skiing in Tuckerman Ravine

No history of skiing in New England is complete without a look back at what has been going on in the bowl at Tuck's for the last six decades.

Mount Washington was first skied from the summit in 1913 via what is now the Auto Road. It was not until the spring of 1926 that AMC hutmaster Joe Dodge and several of his friends ventured into Tuckerman Ravine on skis, skinning up and skiing the snowfields low on the headwall. Among this first crew was Al Sise and his brother Herb. Sise, who is well into his eighties as of this writing and still races in masters' races today, recalls of his first trips into the bowl, "We were intimidated by the ravine. It was a mighty impressive place—awe inspiring." Former AMC Ski Committee chair William Fowler proclaimed on a radio show in 1934, "When we consider that this past summer people skied on the headwall of Tuckerman's as late as July 4th, we realize that it is one of the seven wonders of New Hampshire, rivaling the Great Stone Face and the Flume."

Sise can remember the time when "there was nobody there—not a soul except us" in the ravine; this was soon to change. The first skiers told their friends, who promptly told other skiers about the vast and challenging skiing in the ravine. These first skiers to journey to the ravine had to bushwhack the 2.5 miles to Hermit Lake up the Cutler River drainage. As traffic into the ravine increased, AMC volunteers and the U.S. Forest Service were finally prompted to construct the Fire Trail from Pinkham Notch to Hermit Lake in late 1932. This trail is still the main route to the bowl and is now known as the Tuckerman Ravine Trail. The construction of the Sherburne Trail in 1934 made access to the ravine even easier, allowing skiers to ski from Hermit Lake to Pinkham Notch in under thirty minutes. Providing easy access to the bowl was a turning point in the history of skiing in Tuckerman Ravine.

By the early 1930s, the word about Tuckerman Ravine was out. In 1930 the AMC ran its first ski trip to Tuck's. In April 1931 Dartmouth Outing Club skiers John Carleton (U.S. Olympic ski team, 1924) and Charlie Proctor (U.S. Olympic ski team, 1928 and 1936) became the first to ski over the lip of the headwall down to the ravine floor. By 1932 the snow trains from Boston to New Hampshire were ferrying more than ten thousand people per season to the north country, and many of them were coming to ski in Tuckerman Ravine.

In 1933 the first of three "American Inferno" races were held in the ravine. It was reported in the June 1933 edition of the AMC journal *Appalachia*:

> The climax of the ski racing season this year was also another step in the conquest of Mt. Washington under winter-time conditions. Up until this year the headwall of Tuckerman Ravine, which is a drop of nearly a thousand feet, had been run by only a handful of people, . . . but this spring the snow was so unusually deep in the bowl that the angle was perceptibly less and the Ski Club Hochgebirge of Boston [which counted among its members some of the best racers of the era] thought the time was ripe to conduct a race they had had in mind for some time—a summit-to-base run, including the headwall. They christened it the "American Inferno," after a famous course at Murren, Switzerland.

The race was won by Hollis Phillips of the AMC with a time of 14 minutes, 41 seconds, with most of the other ten skiers finishing in about 20 minutes.

Skiing the Inferno was an amazing accomplishment even by today's standards. The race course dropped 4,200 feet in about 4 miles. The first race started from the summit of Mount Washington, dropped into the ravine via the Right Gully, and skied to Pinkham Notch on the narrow Fire Trail.

The increasing traffic into Tuckerman Ravine was also reflected in the pushing of skiing standards. The Inferno was the best gauge of this. In the second Inferno, held in 1934, legendary Dartmouth racer Dick Durrance astounded the skiing community by winning in 12 minutes, 35 seconds. But the most famous race ever held in the ravine was the third American Inferno, held in 1939.

Toni Matt was an unknown in the American skiing world. A nineteen-year-old Austrian, he had just been brought to the States to teach at the Cranmore Mountain Ski School in North Conway. He had never heard of Tuckerman Ravine, but when told about the race there, he was game to enter. The race was postponed on account of bad weather twice but was finally run on April 19, 1939. The conditions on the summit as the racers waited to be called were 0 degrees with a 60-mph wind. Matt had his first view of the headwall as he climbed up it; he had never seen the Sherburne Trail, which constituted the lower half of the race course. His competitors, especially Durrance of the DOC, were veterans of numerous runs down the mountain.

What occurred next was captured in the race summary that appeared in the December 1939 issue of *Appalachia*:

> An adequate description of Toni Matt's run cannot fail to take your breath away. From below in the ravine, he was seen to come tearing down the cone in one long arc, and with one swoop that was hardly a check he dropped over the lip of the ravine, came straight down the headwall, across the floor, and on down the brook bed to the Sherburne Trail. On the trail he ran with an ease and abandon that left one gasping. He cut

the corners close, never traveling an extra inch. His time of
6:29:2 practically halves any previous time, and he finished
looking as fresh as when he left for the ascent four hours before.

Matt finished a full minute ahead of Durrance, who came in
second. He simply took the headwall straight, a feat few have
dared to repeat. Matt has since offered in the way of explanation, "Being nineteen with strong legs, and stupid, was the
right combination at the right time."

The first era of ski exploration in the bowl was in the early
1930s. Skiers from the Dartmouth College ski team would
come every spring. The first descents of Right Gully, Left
Gully, the Chute, Hillman Highway, and the lip occurred
during this period. Hillman Highway was named for Harry
Hillman, a Dartmouth skier who enjoyed exploring the less-
traveled areas. Sel Hannah, a well-known local skier of the
era and member of the Dartmouth ski team, recalls, "Hillman
was a colorful, wild guy and a damn good skier. Everybody
would be over on the headwall, but he used to go up there [to
Hillman Highway] all the time and promote it. So eventually
a lot of other guys went over there too." Hannah, for his part,
was responsible for the first descent down the center of the
headwall in 1937–38.

The next major era of exploration in the ravine was between 1946 and 1952. Brooks Dodge, son of AMC huts manager Joe Dodge, had the good fortune to live in Pinkham
Notch and was responsible for the bulk of this new activity.
Dodge was also a member of the Dartmouth ski team and a
two-time Olympic ski team member (1952 and 1956). He
made first descents of ten different routes, most of them characterized by being frighteningly steep. Dodge's Drop, which is
just left of the left chute at the top of Hillman Highway, was
named for him and is one of his best-known routes. Among
others he was responsible for are the Dutchess (just right of
Hillman; he says it had been skied once before him), Cathedral (left of Dodge's Drop), Lion's Head gullies 1, 2, and 3
(gullies between Right Gully and Lion's Head), the Sluice

(just above Lunch Rocks), Boott Spur gullies 1, 2, and 3, and the Chute Variation. He claims that his most difficult run was the Icefall, a route down the center of the headwall which forms only occasionally; it has apparently only been skied one other time as of this writing.

For an excellent pictorial history of the early skiing on Mount Washington, see *Mount Washington in Winter: Photographs and Recollections, 1923–1940,* by skier and photographer Winston Pote.

Ski Routes in Tuckerman Ravine

Skiing in Tuckerman Ravine today is as exciting and heartstopping as it ever was. The sensation of climbing the headwall and standing at the top with your heart pounding fast as you try to talk yourself into dropping into the fall line is repeated with each run and each step higher you take.

All the ski routes in Tuckerman Ravine are for expert Nordic skiers and alpine skiers. The prime skiing season in the ravine runs from mid- to late March to around Memorial Day. Skiing usually continues through June and sometimes even until the Fourth of July, but late-season conditions can be difficult.

The most useful source of information about skiing in the ravine, aside from talking with other skiers, is a free, single-page pamphlet entitled *Skiing in Tuckerman Ravine,* issued by the U.S. Forest Service. It includes an aerial photograph of the ravine with most of the popular routes labeled. It is available at the Trading Post at the AMC Pinkham Notch Camp. Descriptions of several of the more popular runs in the Tuckerman Ravine area follow.

The most distinctive feature in the ravine is the headwall. The headwall has a vertical drop of 800 feet from the lip to the floor of the ravine. The headwall gets progressively steeper as you climb it, starting out at 30 degrees at the bottom, rising to 40 degrees just below the lip (at the rock ledge protruding just left of center), and reaching about 50 degrees at the lip. Above the lip are the gentle grades of the Alpine Garden and the moderately steep snowfields on the summit cone.

Several critical factors influence the difficulty and location of skiing in Tuckerman Ravine. Snow conditions, the hour of day, the depth of the corn snow, the firmness of the base, and the runout below a given route (in case of a fall) should all be taken into consideration when deciding where to ski in the bowl. The steepness of each route varies from year to year depending on snow depth.

The most popular runs on the headwall also vary each year, depending on snow conditions throughout the ravine. A usual favorite ascends the right side of the headwall above Lunch Rocks to the lip. Lunch Rocks are the large boulders on the lower right side of the headwall. They are the gathering spot (or bleachers, as they have been called), for the vocal crowd of spectators and skiers who cheer on each skier and applaud the antics of people on the headwall. On a busy weekend, you will see people coming down the headwall on everything from downhill skis, telemark skis, and snowboards, to rubber inner tubes, rubber boats, plastic sleds, and rear ends. A circus? You bet. But it is nevertheless one of the great institutions of New England skiing.

Left Gully climbs to the lip just left of the main headwall. It is a narrow chute that demands quick turning. The grade is extremely steep at the top (about 55 degrees) and gets slightly less severe past the bottleneck in the gully.

Hillman Highway sees less traffic since it is out of the bowl proper. It is the longest of the routes in the area, with a vertical drop of 1,500 feet. It averages about 50 feet in width, opening up to twice that at its widest point. The left fork (when climbing up the gully) at the top of Hillman is the steepest section of the run, approaching 43 degrees. The grade on the right fork is slightly less steep.

Hillman Highway has a distinctly alpine quality and has spectacular views from the top. The run can be reached by climbing up from the bottom from the trail that leaves HoJo's (the caretaker and information hut at Hermit Lake), or by dropping down from the top after reaching the ridge via another route. The top of Hillman is just beyond a rescue cache that is kept in a cylindrical, corrugated steel container just east of the Davis Path. It is possible to hike between Hillman and the headwall on the Davis Path. Be prepared for severe weather if you plan to be up on the ridge.

More moderate skiing around the summit area of Mount Washington can usually be found on the East Snowfields. They are the large, east-facing snowfields that lead up to the summit. They can be reached by climbing up the headwall over the lip, or more commonly, by ascending Right Gully.

Table 2 offers a statistical picture of the ski routes in Tuckerman Ravine.

Part of the experience of spring skiing in Tuckerman Ravine is being part of the community of people who ski there. This is not the place to go if you're looking for a solitary wilderness skiing experience. On a good spring weekend, five thousand people will pass by HoJo's, the meeting place and information center for skiers that lies about half a mile below the floor of the ravine. For people interested in camping out, there are eight shelters at Hermit Lake with room for eighty-six people. They are filled on a first-come, first-served basis. This means they are usually full by Friday night on spring weekends. Camping is forbidden anywhere else in the area.

Table 2
Select Ski Routes in Tuckerman Ravine

Area	Length of Run	Vertical Drop (ft.)	Maximum Pitch (degrees)
Hillman Highway	0.5–0.6 mile	1,500	40
Lower Snowfield	0.2–0.3 mile	700	35
Little Headwall	75 yards	150	35
Left Gully	0.25 mile	800	55
Headwall	0.1–0.2 mile	800	50
Right Gully	0.25 mile	800	40
Sherburne Trail	2.4 miles	1,900	35
East Snowfield	200 yd.	400	30

Source: U.S. Forest Service and Brooks Dodge (interview).

A few words of caution about skiing in Tuckerman Ravine:

- There is often significant danger of avalanche in the ravine and on all surrounding gullies early in the winter or just after a large snowstorm. Check the posted avalanche warnings in Pinkham Notch or at HoJo's. The final assessment of the avalanche hazard, particularly when it is early in the season, rests with each skier. Do not ski if you are uncertain about the stability of the slope—people have been killed or seriously injured by avalanches in the ravine.

- Beware of falling rock or ice on warm days.

- Give crevasses a wide berth when skiing or climbing near them.

- Do not wear slick nylon clothing when skiing, because the reduced friction on snow makes it more difficult to stop sliding.

- If you fall when skiing, get your skis downhill and try to stop yourself by driving the tip of your pole or your hands into the snow.

- Wear sunglasses, sunscreen, and lip protection. Serious sunburn is a common problem, especially during the spring.

Easy Day Trips in the White Mountains

A variety of easier backcountry ski trails have been developed in the White Mountains. Although they do not qualify as classic routes, they deserve special mention for novice skiers who are interested in skiing off the beaten path. They are listed here in an effort to introduce beginning cross-country skiers to the world of backcountry skiing and to entice them into continuing their explorations.

The U.S. Forest Service (USFS) has been active in building a network of moderate backcountry ski trails. The Nanamocomuck Trail and the Oliverian Brook Trails off the Kancamagus Highway (NH 112), the Beaver Brook Trail on NH 3 near Twin Mountain, and the Hayes Copp Ski Trail on NH 16 north of Pinkham Notch are some of the better trails. The Forest Service publishes pamphlets with sketch maps about these and other trails. This information is available from any White Mountain National Forest ranger station or information office, or by contacting the Forest Supervisor, White Mountain National Forest, P.O. Box 638, Laconia, NH 03247 (603-524-6450).

Another beautiful backcountry tour over easy terrain is the Wild River Trail from Jackson to the USFS Hastings Campground on ME 113. The route is heavily used by snowmobiles on its northeastern end, which makes for fast, flat skiing. The trail is most easily accessed for day trips by driving as far south on ME 113 as it is plowed. From where you park your car, you may either ski in alongside the Wild River, or ski south on the unplowed section of ME 113 through Evans Notch. The scenic Wild River has been designated a Wild and Scenic River by the U.S. Congress, assuring that it will be preserved in its free-running state.

Skiing alongside the Wild River on the Wild River Trail.

The Appalachian Mountain Club has developed an excellent network of backcountry ski trails near its Pinkham Notch headquarters on NH 16. The Blanchard Loop, the Square Ledge Loop, and the Lost Pond Trail are several of the popular easy tours. *Ski Touring in Pinkham Notch* is a free pamphlet, available from the AMC, which describes and rates a dozen trails.

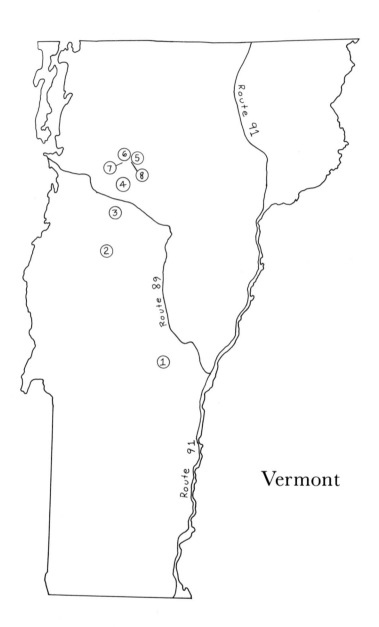

Vermont

Part III

VERMONT

A Note on Maps. A variety of high-quality maps cover Vermont. USGS maps for the area are recent issues in the 7.5-minute series. Northern Cartographic publishes the *Stowe Cross-Country Ski Map.* The Green Mountain Club (GMC) publishes annotated maps of Mount Mansfield and Camel's Hump; they are included with the GMC *Guide Book of the Long Trail* or can be purchased separately in some outdoor stores and from the GMC. See the bibliography for additional information on maps.

Skyline Trail

THE TOUR   The Skyline Trail travels a scenic ridge through rural central Vermont, crossing numerous farms and pasture lands.

LENGTH   6.3 miles

ELEVATION   Starting: 1,600 feet; high point: 1,700 feet; ending: 700 feet

MAPS   USGS Woodstock North (7.5-minute series, 1966), available at the Woodstock Ski Touring Center, Woodstock. A Skyline Trail pamphlet, including a sketch map and route description, is also available at the touring center. Note that the Skyline Trail is not included on the USGS map.

DIFFICULTY   Moderate

HOW TO GET THERE   From the town of Woodstock, take VT 12 north, bearing right after 0.7 mile and following the signs to the Suicide Six ski area. Leave one car at Suicide Six, turn right out of the parking lot and drive 0.25 mile to South Pomfret, where you turn left (north) on the County Road. Drive 5 miles to Hewitt's Corner and turn left at a road junction where there is a sign for Sharon. Go 0.2 mile, then turn left again on a dirt road. Go straight north-northwest on this road about 2 miles until it bends to the right and ascends a hill. Park at the top of the hill in the plowed parking pullout on the east side of the road (if you begin descending the hill, you have gone too far). There are blue trail markers and signs for a "natural area" on the west side of the road which may be partly obscured by the snowbank. This is the start of the Skyline Trail.

Skiing past a farmhouse in rural Vermont on the Skyline Trail.

The Skyline Trail near Woodstock may do more to capture the spirit of New England than any other ski tour. It offers views that can be found only in the heart of Vermont. The rolling pastures and farmhouses that it skirts will bring a warm smile of familiarity to old-time New Englanders. Newcomers to the area will get a quick introduction to what it is about this part of the world that keeps people coming back throughout their lives. The Skyline Trail is as much a tour of rural New England as it is an enjoyable backcountry ski experience.

The Skyline Trail exists thanks to the courtesy of more than twenty private landowners whose permission was secured. Credit for envisioning this trail and persuading these neighbors to allow access to their land goes to Richard Brett, a former resident of Woodstock who owned property in Barnard. Brett was eager to build a ski route that would connect his two homes. In the 1960s he began exploring where the route might go and asking local residents if he could blaze a trail through their land. He connected a series of logging roads, abandoned roads, and clearings in order to minimize the amount of new trail cutting that he would have to do. His original plan to connect Barnard with Woodstock never materialized fully. The section from Barnard to Amity Pond is a steep uphill climb that few skiers bother including, and efforts to cut a trail from the Suicide Six ski area, where the trail now ends, to Woodstock have been unsuccessful.

The most commonly skied sections of the trail proceed from the town of Barnard south for 6.3 miles to South Pomfret. A car shuttle must be done beforehand. Drop one car at the Suicide Six ski area and head out in another car to the trailhead. That's where the fun starts. The trickiest navigation on this ski tour may be just finding the trailhead. If you've ever laughed at the frustrated attempts of a flatlander to navigate his or her way around rural New England, you may find that the joke is on you on this day. Just a few miles outside of touristy, bustling Woodstock, you are in the New England outback. Dirt roads dart off in every direction (except the one you are expecting), streets are never marked, locals have never heard of the place you looking for, and you soon doubt

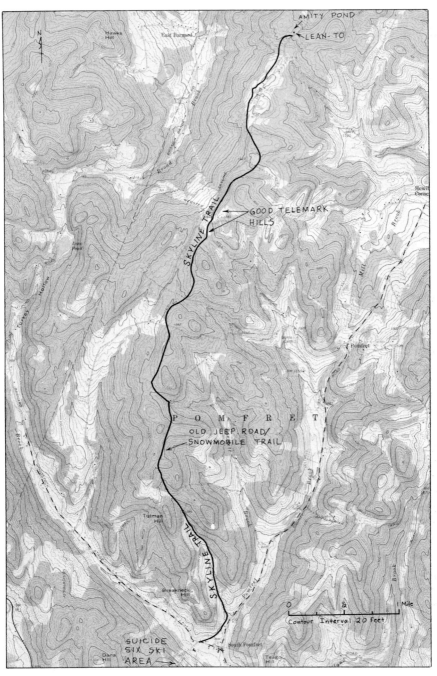

Skyline Trail

whether you can, in fact, get from the proverbial "he-ah" to "they-ah."

There is a lean-to just in from the road at the trail's start at Amity Pond. Originally built by Brett, this shelter has since been rebuilt. A letter posted inside it expresses Brett's sentiments: "This campsite is a place to go to escape the din and cacophony of towns and cities, roads and highways. It has been a retreat from the trials of day to day endeavors and it has been a place to enjoy the intimacy of true companionship and nature." Camping is allowed in the lean-to on a first-come, first-served basis.

Just north of the lean-to is Amity Pond. According to local legend, it was so named because two girlhood friends from different nearby towns would come to meet and spend time there. Richard and Elizabeth Brett owned the land and donated it to the state, and it is now preserved as the Amity Pond Natural Area.

The trail continues past the lean-to and opens onto a hill in a wide clearing. This is the first of many open views of the surrounding countryside. The trail continues, crossing wide pastures and stone and wooden fences that mark off past and present property boundaries. These views, the essence of Vermont, are rarely accessed by a backcountry ski trail: a mix of rolling hills, the round peaks of the Green Mountains, isolated farmhouses, and befuddled-looking cows. This is not a "wilderness" trail in the pure sense, and that is part of its appeal. The signs of civilization, such as farmhouses and unplowed roads, lend as much to the ambience and experience of this ski tour as open hardwoods do to a remote mountainside.

The trail meanders over pastures and into woods, passing through tunnel-like stands of red pine in the first 2 miles. The trail plays around, darting up and dropping off an intermittent 1,700-foot ridge. The route crosses at least four roads. This is typical of New England, where every valley had a road built through it at the time it was settled.

Where the trail crosses the Webster Hill Road (plowed), broad, open hills flank the road. It is a perfect place to stop and carve some telemark turns. The trail continues for 1.7 miles to where it joins an old jeep road. This is the beginning of a fast 2-mile descent. This final section of trail is also used by snowmobilers. Be courteous about sharing the path. Halfway down the jeep road, skiers can stop and climb Totman Hill to the west, where good views of the surrounding ski area and towns are visible. The trail drops more than 700 feet in the final 2 miles before crossing a field and ending at Suicide Six.

The staff at the Woodstock Ski Touring Center is committed to maintaining the Skyline Trail as an ungroomed, nonfee backcountry ski trail. John Wiggin, director of the ski touring center, explained that they maintain it as a public service. They feel that it is in keeping with the spirit of backcountry skiing that people should not have to pay for the experience of skiing ungroomed trails. Many backcountry enthusiasts hope that this rarely heard sentiment catches on with other ski touring center operators.

Other Options. The official Skyline Trail begins in East Barnard. Smaller loops or a 2-mile climb may be tacked onto the route described here. Details of this section of the trail are available in the Skyline Trail pamphlet, available at the Woodstock Touring Center.

Long Trail

THE TOUR   The Monroe Skyline section of the Long Trail as it traverses the high, narrow ridge between Appalachian Gap and Lincoln Gap near Waitsfield

LENGTH   Appalachian Gap (VT 17) to Lincoln Gap (Lincoln-Warren Highway): 11.6 miles; Lincoln Peak (Sugarbush/South Basin ski area) to Stark Mountain (Mad River Glen ski area): 5.7 miles

ELEVATION   High point: 4,083 feet (Mount Ellen); low point: 2,365 feet (Appalachian Gap)

MAPS   The USGS Mount Ellen quadrangle (7.5-minute series, 1971) covers Lincoln Peak to Appalachian Gap; the USGS Lincoln quadrangle (7.5-minute series, 1970) covers Lincoln Gap. Maps are available in Waitsfield at the Tempest Bookshop.

DIFFICULTY   More difficult

HOW TO GET THERE   From Waitsfield, the Mad River Glen ski area is about 5 miles west on VT 17, and Appalachian Gap is accessible by car just up the road from the ski area. Sugarbush/South Basin is 6 miles south of Waitsfield on VT 100. The Lincoln-Warren Highway, which leaves west shortly after the turnoff for Sugarbush, is usually only plowed up to 1.1 miles before Lincoln Gap; the rest of the way must be skied.

The Long Trail runs the length of Vermont, from the Massachusetts to the Canadian border, a total of 265 miles. It is a rugged footpath through some of the most interesting and

Threading through the trees on the Long Trail.

scenic terrain in Vermont. It has many shelters for overnight use that are managed by the Green Mountain Club.

The section of the Long Trail from Appalachian Gap to Lincoln Gap just west of Waitsfield is one of the most spectacular sections of the entire trail. From Lincoln Peak to Stark Mountain (also referred to as General Stark Mountain in the GMC *Guide Book of the Long Trail*), a distance of nearly 6 miles, the trail follows the crest of an exposed narrow ridge as it climbs and dips between 3,400 and 4,000 feet in elevation. Between Lincoln Gap and Appalachian Gap the trail traverses the summit of two of the five mountains in Vermont that are over 4,000 feet, Mount Ellen (4,083 feet, third highest in the state) and Mount Abraham (4,006 feet), and also Cutts Peak (4,022 feet), one of five peaks on Lincoln Mountain. The trail was laid in 1913 by a state crew, which cut a swath all the way from Camel's Hump to Lincoln Gap in one concerted ax-wielding push. That entire section of the Long Trail became known as the Monroe Skyline, in honor of a retired professor who spent his later years living on the east side of Camel's Hump. It was through Monroe's efforts that a number of trails in this area were built.

The Mad River valley has long been known by local skiers to be a snow pocket. The prominent north-south ridge that forms the western border of the valley benefits from being the first large mountain ridge east of Lake Champlain, catching the brunt of wet storms from the west. In the 1960s, ski pioneer Roland Palmedo, the founder of the Mad River Glen ski area, spent time cutting and blazing his own ski routes on the north end of the ridge near Appalachian Gap. Skiers can still find his blazes, made from tin can lids, scattered around on trees in the area near Stark Mountain.

Palmedo was enchanted with this ridge. "Scenically, this portion of the Long Trail is unsurpassed," he wrote in the December 1951 *Appalachia* after skiing from Appalachian Gap to Lincoln Gap. "The ridge being as sharp as a church roof most of the way, one can frequently look down on the parallel valleys on either side. . . . the area is one of the wildest and most unspoiled in the state."

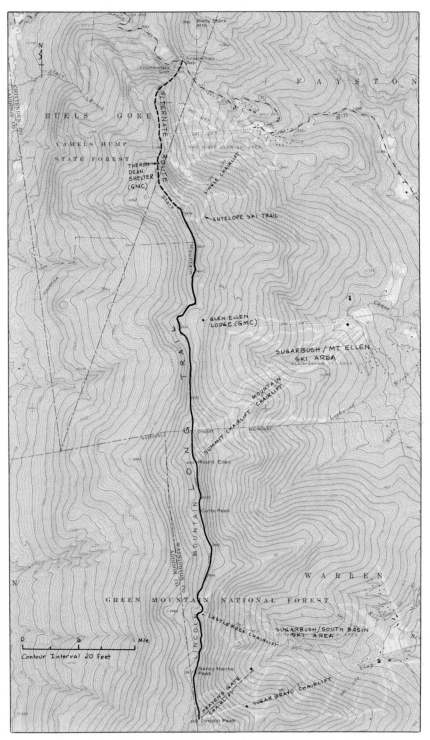

Long Trail

Today, two thriving ski areas inhabit the valley: Mad River Glen and Sugarbush. Sugarbush consists of two main areas. South Basin refers to the trails on Lincoln Peak, and Mount Ellen encompasses the trails on the mountain of the same name.

Most people prefer to ski the section of ridge between the Mad River Glen and Sugarbush ski areas. Both Lincoln Gap and Appalachian Gap are steep notches accessed by narrow trails that are difficult to ski. From Appalachian Gap, the trail climbs 800 feet in 0.5 mile to where it attains the ridge. From Lincoln Gap, the ascent is 1,600 feet in 2.6 miles. A trip from gap to gap is best done as an overnight, staying at one of the three GMC shelters on the route.

To access the ridge from the Mad River Glen ski area, take the single chair and exit to the left (south), heading down to the Antelope ski trail. The entrance to the Long Trail will appear shortly on the right and is indicated by a sign. From Sugarbush/South Basin, take the Heaven's Gate Triple Chair (accessed by taking the Sugar Bravo Chairlift and skiing part of the Downspout Trail) to the summit. At the top of the lift there is a small knob of land, the top of which is the summit of Lincoln Peak. Sidestep up, and the entrance to the Long Trail is just off to the south. The entrance is obscure and there is no sign, but the opening is blazed with a painted white slash. The trail can be tricky to follow at the start, since nearby ski area trails run parallel to it. Within a half mile the ridge becomes narrow enough that all trails along its top merge.

Several considerations are involved in deciding whether to ski the ridge north to south or vice versa. There is generally an equal amount of uphill and downhill skiing whichever way you take. However, Sugarbush does not sell single-ride lift tickets, meaning you either have to ski up the mountain or purchase a hefty full-price ticket. Mad River Glen does sell single-ride lift tickets.

If you aren't already familiar with the mystique of Mad River Glen, buying a lift ticket and taking part of a morning to explore the famous glades and "off-trail trails" of this mountain is well worth it. Mad River is much loved by a large community of skiers in the East who see it as one of the last "skier's mountains." There is no "out of bounds" here, no glitz, and minimal snowmaking. This is skiing as it used to be: a mountain where you can pick your favorite line and ski it to the bottom, regardless of whether it happens to be on the trail map. The woods skiing in the valley surrounding the mountain includes some of the best powder runs you could ask for, and if you like moguls, the trail system on the mountain is guaranteed to humble you. Telemarkers flock to Mad River, which partly accounts for the popularity of the annual eastern telemark festival held there every March by the North American Telemark Organization (see appendix A).

Assuming a few good runs at Mad River haven't caused you to abandon your plan to ski the ridge, you are in for an enjoyable alpine experience. The trail rises and falls along the 3,600-foot ridge of Stark Mountain, dropping steeply before passing the junction with the Jerusalem Trail and descending again to a saddle between Stark Mountain and Mount Ellen. A hint for confused map readers is in order here: Stark Mountain is the location of Mad River Glen, Mount Ellen is the location of the trails of Sugarbush/Mount Ellen, and Nancy Hanks Peak and Lincoln Peak are both part of Sugarbush/South Basin.

The Long Trail can be followed through the woods so that there is no need to enter the trail system of Sugarbush/Mount Ellen, with the exception of a few hundred feet north of the highest chairlift. However, if skiing south to north, the Long Trail can also be accessed from an entrance off the Exterminator ski trail. Continuing south an "LT South" sign marks the reentry point to the woods just behind the upper station of the Summit Double Chair. Climbing up past the Summit Double Chair to the 4,083-foot summit of Mount Ellen, the route is more straightforward as it follows the narrow ridge.

The skiing from Mount Ellen to Sugarbush/South Basin is marked by tight turns and short, fast downhill shots, interspersed with skiing up and down some small ridge knolls. At one point, the Long Trail connects briefly with a Sugarbush ski trail as it passes the Castle Rock Chairlift. The entrance back into the woods is marked by a sign just past the chair. Skiers can opt to end the tour at the South Basin ski trails by dropping down a trail served by the Castle Rock Chairlift, or continue another mile to Lincoln Peak and end on a trail that leads down from there.

Part of what make this ski tour a classic are the alpine setting and the scenery. Throughout the length of the ridge, numerous overlooks and clearings offer long views all the way to the Adirondacks in the west, and clear into the Northeast Kingdom of Vermont in the northeast. From the southern section of the trail near Sugarbush/South Basin, it is possible to see Mount Marcy to the west, the White Mountains 80 miles to the east, and Killington Peak in the south.

Skiing this route is a serious undertaking. If you are not comfortable skiing downhill through narrow slots and making quick turns, this ski tour is probably not for you. There are also some mountaineering considerations to take into account. Weather can move in very fast, in which case you are in a poor position to seek shelter. Skiing this route will probably take longer than you think, since route finding can be tricky. The white trail blazes are often painted low to the ground and become covered by snow, due to the fact that the Long Trail is not maintained as a ski trail. Skiers should be comfortable navigating by map and compass, and should be carrying both. The best advice for staying on route is to let the topography guide you. Generally the trail follows the top of the ridge, although it wanders back and forth along it in places. If you begin descending off either side of the ridge, you are going the wrong way. This is also a fairly remote tour, and your party should be equipped to deal with any contingency.

One hazard deserves special mention on this route. With 5–10 feet or more of snow on this summer hiking trail, you are basically skiing through the tops of the trees. Spikey spruce and fir branches crowd the narrow trail and can easily catch you off guard, causing serious injury. This trail has not been groomed to accommodate skiers; for this reason *wearing eye protection is essential.*

A nice feature of this tour is that there are a number of

places at which you can bail out. The trails of the two Sugar-bush mountains can be used for a quick exit if you are either moving more slowly than you'd planned or if there is a mis-hap. Sugarbush also runs a shuttle bus between its two moun-tains. If you haven't spotted a vehicle at both ends of the route, you can take the free shuttle from Sugarbush/South Basin to Mount Ellen and get a ride the rest of the way to Mad River to retrieve your car.

The words of warning heeded, this is a unique and beauti-ful ski tour. Just being introduced to the area and its numer-ous ski opportunities makes it worth the effort to visit this famous "skier's valley."

Camel's Hump

THE TOUR   The Honey Hollow Trail has a mix of fast downhill sections and flat skiing on gentler logging roads. It is a good introduction to the numerous skiing possibilities on Camel's Hump.

LENGTH   7.5 miles, touring center to River Road

ELEVATION   Starting: 1,500 feet; high point: 2,000 feet; ending: 400 feet

MAPS   The USGS Huntington quadrangle (7.5-minute series, 1980) covers the terrain of the Honey Hollow Trail and the west side of Camel's Hump; the USGS Waterbury quadrangle (7.5-minute series, 1980) covers the east side of Camel's Hump; the USGS Camel's Hump quadrangle (15-minute series, 1948) and Green Mountain Club *Trail Map of Camel's Hump* cover all of Camel's Hump Forest Reserve. None of these maps show the Honey Hollow Trail.

DIFFICULTY   More difficult

FEE   This is a fee trail of the Camel's Hump Nordic Ski Center (802-434-2704).

HOW TO GET THERE   The Camel's Hump Nordic Ski Center is located in Huntington, Vermont. From I-89, take the Richmond exit. Follow the signs to Huntington from the center of Richmond; signs direct you to the ski touring center from Huntington.

Camel's Hump is considered by many Vermont skiers to be the jewel of the state's backcountry skiing areas. While that may be disputed (Mount Mansfield devotees certainly have

Powderhound heaven: skiing a hiking trail on Camel's Hump.

plenty of ammunition to counter the claim), no one would deny that Camel's Hump boasts some of the finest back-country skiing in the East.

What can be so special about such a funny-looking mountain? For starters, it is the only undeveloped high peak in Vermont—that is, it is the only big mountain that you can ski all the way around without running into a chairlift. In Vermont, home to dozens of ski resorts, that counts for a lot. It's not that land speculators haven't fantasized about this mountain. It's just that the state of Vermont, in an effort to repent for its days of development gone wild, declared the summit a Natural Area in 1965 and extended protection to the rest of the mountain in 1969 by making it part of Camel's Hump Forest Reserve.

Camel's Hump is a distinctive land feature, visible from downtown Burlington and from more than 20 miles away as you approach it from the southeast on I-89. Its three-tiered summit cone has always struck me as most closely resembling the profile of a lion; the debate over just what the summit does look like has raged for years. The Green Mountain Club *Guide Book of the Long Trail* recounts the story thus:

> The Waubanaukee Indians called Camel's Hump "the saddled mountain," and Samuel de Champlain's explorers named it "le lion couchant," translated "the Couching (not crouching) Lion." Either name is more descriptive of the mountain's profile when viewed from east or west than is Camel's Hump, a name amended by Zadock Thompson in 1830 from the less genteel "Camel's Rump" listed on Ira Allen's 1798 map.

Camel's Hump has attracted a fiercely loyal following among a small group of skiers from the surrounding area. The reasons for this are simple: the mountain is blessed with an abundance of snow (an average of 220 inches annually) and, most important, is unknown to the vast majority of skiers.

The Honey Hollow Trail is a great appetizer for what

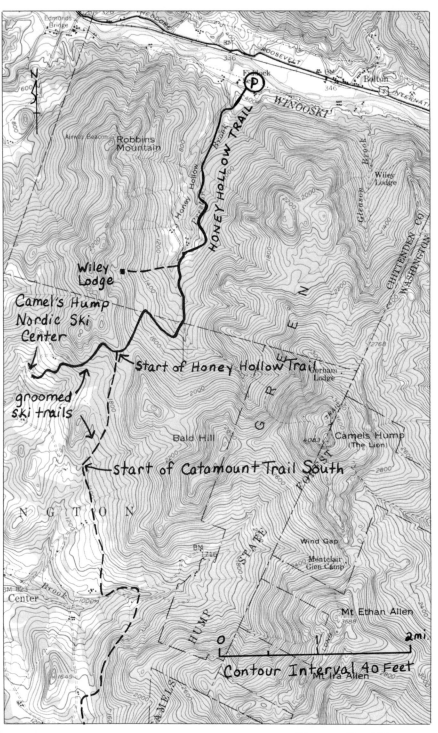

Camel's Hump

Camel's Hump has to offer. The trail, cut in 1980 by Camel's Hump Nordic Ski Center owner Dave Brautigan and state forest rangers, drops 1,500 feet in 5.6 miles and can be a delight in powder. The trail is part of the 280-mile Catamount Trail system (see appendix A for more information). The Honey Hollow is a rollicking trail, with some swooping downhills, that is similar in character to the popular Wildcat Valley Trail in New Hampshire.

The trail is accessed by skiing for 2 miles through the trail system of the Camel's Hump Nordic Ski Center. This requires paying a trail fee at the touring center. This touring center, off the beaten track of the glitzy Vermont ski scene (yes, even cross-country ski centers are succumbing to crowds and designer clothes), is worth a visit on its own. It is perched 1,000 feet above the town of Huntington, with a beautiful view down the Winooski River valley. The touring center offers a wide variety of trails through the rugged woods and hills at the foot of Camel's Hump. Having bought a trail ticket, you can opt to ski on the trail network for a half day before heading down the Honey Hollow Trail.

A car must be spotted at the trail's end on River Road before starting out (see road directions above; the touring center does not offer a shuttle service). You will need a touring center map, given to you when you buy your trail ticket, in order to navigate through the trail system to reach the beginning of Honey Hollow. The most direct route takes the Pond Road Trail from the touring center to Jack's Jog, leading to Woodchuck Ramble, to Logger's Loop, and finally to Honey Hollow. The blue blazes of the Catamount Trail signal the beginning of the route. At the top of the last rise, a clear view to the southeast of the profile of Camel's Hump comes into sight.

The trail begins with some long, straight and narrow downhill chutes, followed by short, steep drops, which alternate with flatter terrain. The trail then follows woods roads through a wide S-turn. It continues dropping alongside Preston Brook, finally taking a sharp right turn and crossing the deep ravine on a bridge. The trail soon crosses the Long Trail (blazed white), which was temporarily rerouted in 1987 at the request of a landowner. The Long Trail now coincides with the Catamount Trail from this point until the end of the Honey Hollow Trail. The route dovetails with logging roads for the rest of its length, heading steadily but more gradually downhill and darting in and out of the woods at various points. The trail ends at River Road. Skiers should note that they must pick up their car back at the touring center by 5:30 P.M. unless they have informed people at the center of other plans. The touring center is obligated to notify the state police in order to begin a search for people who they think may still be out on the trails after dark.

The Honey Hollow Trail has grown in popularity over the past few years and tends to be heavily traveled (often twenty to thirty people) on good weekends. First tracks after a storm will likely be reserved for those who get to it midweek. The accessibility and popularity of the route should not lull people into being unprepared. This ski tour is not suitable for novice skiers, it is not patrolled by the touring center, and there is no easy way out if you decide you are not feeling up to it.

Camel's Hump will not unfold all its skiing secrets on one visit. It is a mountain that can be explored for years, always yielding some new pearl. The best skiing is not even on the trails. It is in the legendary open glades of this mountain, which you may hit upon one day and not be able to discover the next or even describe to someone else. A few hints: the Forest City and Burrows trails on the west side of the mountain, and the Forestry Trail on the east side, access some of the best glade skiing on the mountain. There is also excellent skiing on other hiking trails.

The most important requirement for skiing off-trail on Camel's Hump is a sense of adventure and days when you're not in a hurry. Stories abound of people wandering off a trail and skiing for miles through birch and hardwood glades, always ending with a big smile on their faces in some place they never planned on coming out. Such is the happy-go-lucky spirit of this special mountain.

Bolton-Trapp Traverse

THE TOUR   A ski route from the Bolton Valley Ski Touring Center to the Nebraska Valley Road near Stowe, with the option of continuing into the Trapp Family Ski Touring Center trail network and ending at the famous Trapp Family Lodge

LENGTH   Bolton to Nebraska Valley Road: 8.3 miles; Bolton to Trapp Family Lodge: 11.8 miles

ELEVATION   Starting: 2,000 feet; high point, 3,300 feet; Nebraska Valley Road trailhead: 1,000 feet

MAPS   USGS Bolton Mountain (7.5-minute series, 1948); *Stowe Cross-Country Ski Map,* Northern Cartographic

DIFFICULTY   More difficult

FEE   A reduced trail fee is charged by the Bolton Valley Ski Touring Center for use of its trail system to access this route.

HOW TO GET THERE   Take the Bolton exit off I-89 and follow the signs to Bolton Valley ski area. Bolton Valley Ski Touring Center is at the north end of the parking lots.

The ski tour between the Bolton Valley Ski Touring Center and the Nebraska Valley Road travels through the heart of Vermont ski country. The Green Mountains in this region are speckled with downhill ski areas, obvious to anyone who drives the roads in this area during the winter. This region is well endowed with ski areas because of to the abundance of snow that falls here and the quality of the mountain skiing.

Telemarking through a birch glade near the start of the Bolton Trapp Traverse.

The Bolton-Trapp Traverse (also known as the Bolton-to-Stowe Trail) offers backcountry skiers some of the pleasures of this area that downhill skiers have been enjoying for years. One of the things that makes it a classic ski tour is the wide variety of terrain that it covers. Beginning at the groomed trails of the Bolton Valley Ski Touring Center, the trail travels through a wild, high-mountain environment and offers the option of ending at one of New England's most famous cross-country skiing centers.

An added attraction is the fact that this trail is part of the Catamount Trail, a 280-mile backcountry ski trail that runs the entire length of Vermont. Along its course, the Catamount Trail links some two dozen ski touring centers (see appendix A for more information on the Catamount Trail).

The only drawback of this tour is the fact that a time-consuming, 35-mile car shuttle between Bolton and Stowe must be done. One solution is to have friends who want to ski downhill on Mount Mansfield drop you off in Bolton; by the time their day of skiing is over and they drive to the Trapp Family Lodge or the Nebraska Valley Road, you should just be finishing.

The idea of linking the Bolton and Trapp Family touring centers belonged to Johannes von Trapp, the founder of the Trapp Family Touring Center. Von Trapp spoke with Gardner Lane, who was a moving force behind the Bolton Valley Ski Touring Center, and they decided to undertake a joint effort to link their respective trail networks with an ambitious, over-the-mountain backcountry ski route. In the spring of 1972, the two men, each accompanied by a trail crew, flagged and cut their way up opposite sides of Bolton Mountain. They used old logging roads and abandoned trails wherever possible.

Von Trapp, now in charge of the Trapp family businesses, describes himself as someone who "skis to get out into the woods more than for the sake of skiing." In the early 1970s, he imagined that the future of cross-country skiing would be ski touring in the backcountry, and that the Bolton-Trapp Trail would become a centerpiece of the Trapp family ski trail net-

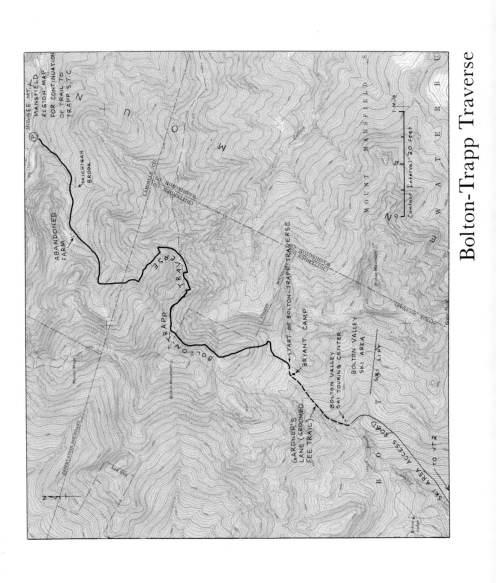

Bolton-Trapp Traverse

work. This turned out to be wishful thinking. Skiers have flocked to the groomed trails of touring centers and have only recently returned to the mountains on Nordic skis.

The route begins at the Bolton Valley Ski Touring Center, which has its headquarters in a small hut located just beyond the condos at the Bolton Valley ski resort near the town of Bolton. Starting the route from the Stowe side would make most of the route an uphill climb. Don't be deterred if you don't see a lot of snow on the ground on your drive in to Bolton. The north-facing slopes on this route accumulate and hold good quantities of snow.

Since the trail begins at the Bolton Valley Ski Touring Center, you are asked to purchase a reduced-fee trail ticket before heading out. Also, the folks here are a useful source of information on route conditions.

Leaving the touring center, make your first right onto the Gardner's Lane Trail. The trail rises gradually and is generously marked with orange flashing. Passing through a spruce and fir meadow, you will have views of the ski resort and the lift lines behind you, just in case you forgot why you decided to abandon the crowds for the day.

You can stop at the small Bryant Camp hut for a break. It is the last outpost of civilization before the trail heads up into the hills. Finding the beginning of the trail after this can be a bit tricky. At the Bryant Camp trail junction, follow the signs to Birch Grove/Heavenly Highway—you will quickly see a blue plastic Catamount Trail blaze in front of you. Several hundred yards past this intersection, the trail enters a small meadow. The Devil's Delight and Heavenly Highway trails leave uphill to the right, and the Bolton-Trapp Trail continues straight ahead on flat ground, although the junction is not clearly marked as of this writing. About 0.2 mile beyond this junction, there is another junction, with blue Catamount Trail blazes going off to the right to mark the way to an ungroomed trail. A sign announces the beginning of the traverse. The route is clearly marked from here on with blue plastic Catamount Trail blazes and red plastic blazes.

The trail quickly climbs into an open grove of birches, with wide-open eastern panoramas of the Green Mountains. Don't resist the temptation to telemark through the glades here— God didn't put the spaces between those trees for nothing! The trail then takes a moderate climb up a ridge, contouring below the summit of Bolton Mountain (elevation 3,725 feet) through an area with a good deal of blowdown. After a series of short, steep climbs and drops, the trail swings around to the east, following along the top of a shoulder of the mountain which runs east-southeast. Be prepared for exposure to the full force of the elements up here; the trees are small and provide little protection from the wind. If you do get hammered by weather while you are up here, you can take some comfort in knowing that the trail soon drops off sharply to the north, providing a good degree of shelter.

Skiing down is a delight in good conditions. The forest is fairly open, and the Michigan Brook drainage that the trail descends is often a powder basin. Several skiers can ski alongside each other, choosing their slots through the trees at will, dovetailing with the trail when it suits them. No one need follow in anyone else's tracks. If you like what you find up high, you will have reason to think you might have a good day of skiing: there are 6 more miles of steady but moderate downhill in which to play.

When the conditions in this north-facing drainage are icy, the trail is arduous and dangerous and probably not worth skiing. It is best to get information on trail conditions at the Bolton Valley Ski Touring Center before heading out.

The trail crosses a number of stream drainages, which may be open if there is light snow cover or if it is late in the season. After taking some wide switchbacks through the forest and crossing Michigan Brook, the trail parallels the brook the remainder of the route to the Nebraska Valley Road. The trail drops down quickly and passes a small wooden house on the right. The house is used by a girls' camp in the summer. The trail soon enters a large clearing. This was the site of a farm in the 1930s and 1940s. The trail cuts left here, following an abandoned town road that once served the farm. It is a steady downhill from here to the trailhead.

Michigan Brook (unnamed on the map) is worth stopping to look at as you ski alongside it on the old town road. It constricts into a narrow gorge and has a waterfall near the old farm site, then continues as a boulder-choked stream down into the Nebraska Valley.

Once at Nebraska Valley Road, you have two choices. You may end at this point, provided you have made arrangements to meet a car here, or you may continue into the network of trails of the Trapp Family Ski Touring Center, which lead to the center's main buildings. This latter section can be difficult to follow; it is not unheard of for skiers to negotiate the backcountry traverse successfully, only to get lost in this little-used part of the Trapp trail system!

To continue to the Trapp Family Ski Touring Center, you must take your skis off and walk left, up the road, for 0.1 mile. A few strategically placed blue plastic blazes continue to mark the way. Old County Road (incorrectly labeled as "Old Country Road" on the *Stowe Cross-Country Ski Map*) is the plowed road that leaves to your right at the top of a rise. You must turn right and walk 0.7 mile on the road. When you reach a house on the left and an open field across the street on the right, a trail (actually the continuation of the original Old County Road) leads off to the right, with blazes marking the beginning of it. This is the Old County Road Trail of the Trapp system. The blazes end here, and the *Stowe Cross-Country Ski Map* is not terribly accurate either. After crossing a wooden bridge and passing a small house on the right, the trail continues but has captured a stream, forcing you to cross from side to side. The trail ends after a mile on a large, open knoll where it intersects with the Russell Knoll Track of the Trapp system. From here, it is about 1.5 miles via the Russell Knoll Track to the parking lot at the Trapp Family Ski Touring Center. The touring center has agreed to waive the trail fee for skiers who just use their trails to exit from this route.

This is a committing ski tour. The area between Bolton and Stowe is relatively remote—which is one of the primary attractions of this route. The trail is not groomed and is not patrolled by either the Trapp Family or the Bolton Valley ski touring centers. Skiers on this route should be prepared to bail themselves out of any situation.

Other Options. Skiers can elect to ski only part of the route from either of the touring centers and then backtrack.

Mount Mansfield Region

Mount Mansfield (elevation 4,393 feet) is the highest mountain in Vermont. Viewed from the east and west, the ridgeline of the mountain resembles the profile of a face. Hence, the names given to the various features along the ridge, from south to north: Forehead, Nose, Upper Lip, Lower Lip, Chin, and Adam's Apple. According to the Green Mountain Club *Guide Book of the Long Trail,* the Abenaki Indians originally named the mountain Moze-o-de-be-Wadso ("Mountain-with-the-head-of-a-Moose"), but the current name was adopted from the nearby town of Mansfield, which is now defunct.

Mount Mansfield has caught the eye of skiers since the turn of the century. Many ski trails were cut on both sides of the mountain, beginning in the early 1930s. Many of these trails were incorporated into the network of the Mount Mansfield at Stowe downhill ski area that still thrives on the northeast slopes of the mountain. What the ski area left behind, backcountry skiers can claim today. Mount Mansfield is now home to many of the finest backcountry ski trails in New England. Much of the history of skiing on Mount Mansfield, and indeed in New England, can be found in the history of the ski trails that are described in this section.

The ski tours in the Mount Mansfield region offer a combination of interesting trail skiing and challenging tree skiing. The open forests that remain from the years of heavy logging activity are now an ideal setting for skiers who enjoy weaving through the birches and finding their own lines of descent. The history of skiing in this area and the quality and variety of ski terrain make this entire region an essential destination for skiers in search of the classic New England skiing experience.

A Note on Maps. Neither the USGS Mount Mansfield quad-rangle (7.5-minute series, 1980) nor the Green Mountain Club *Mount Mansfield Area* map show most of the ski trails in the Mount Mansfield region. An excellent annotated map that includes all of the ski trails of the Mount Mansfield region and the Bolton-Trapp Trail is the *Stowe Cross-Country Ski Map*. It is available at the touring centers in Stowe or from Northern Cartographic.

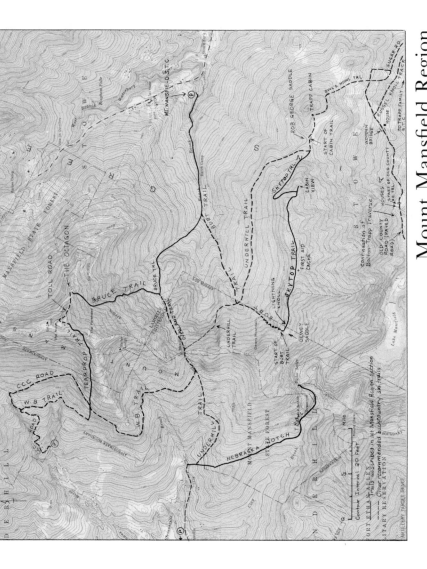

Mount Mansfield Region

Bruce Trail/Teardrop Trail/Nebraska Notch Trail/Skytop Trail

Mount Mansfield Region

Bruce Trail

THE TOUR   The Bruce Trail drops 1,400 feet in just over a mile, making it one of the more exciting backcountry down-mountain ski runs in the Northeast. It is another of the famous CCC ski trails.

LENGTH   2.3 miles to the Burt Trail; 3.5 miles from the Octagon to the Mount Mansfield Touring Center

ELEVATION   Starting: 3,600 feet; ending: 1,000 feet

MAPS   USGS Mount Mansfield (7.5-minute series, 1980); *Stowe Cross-Country Ski Map*, Northern Cartographic; GMC *Mount Mansfield Area* map

DIFFICULTY   Most difficult

FEE   This ungroomed trail is maintained by the Trapp Family and Mount Mansfield touring centers. The purchase of a lift ticket at the Mount Mansfield at Stowe ski area or a trail ticket from one of the cooperating ski touring centers in Stowe is required to ski this route.

HOW TO GET THERE   From the Mount Mansfield at Stowe ski area, take the Forerunner Quad Chairlift to the Octagon. The chairlifts can be used free of charge between 8 A.M. and 9 A.M. The Bruce Trail leaves to the left from just behind (west of) the stone hut.

A skier using the right tool for the job: parallel skiing on the Bruce Trail.

On June 9, 1933, a contingent of the Civilian Conservation Corps, the federal jobs recovery program, arrived in Waterbury, Vermont, just down the road from Mount Mansfield. Vermont State Forester Perry Merrill, himself an avid skier, had just the project for these eager young men: he would have them cut a ski trail from near the summit of Mount Mansfield to the Mountain Road in Stowe. This was to become the Bruce Trail, named for a well-known local lumberman.

The Bruce Trail was an immediate hit with skiers. In February 1934 it was the site of Mount Mansfield's first ski race. The winner won with a time of 10 minutes, 48 seconds; placing second in that race was Charlie Lord, later to become the master designer of Mount Mansfield's downhill trail system. The Bruce Trail and the Nose Dive, which dropped off from the Octagon (a cafeteria and bar at the top of the Forerunner Quad Chairlift) on the opposite side of the Toll Road from the Bruce Trail, formed the nucleus of ski activity on the mountain.

Stowe lumberman and skier Craig Burt, Sr., fixed up an old logging camp and turned it into the ski accommodations known as the Ranch Camp in 1932. Early skiing on the Bruce and other trails on Mount Mansfield was intimately connected with life at the Ranch Camp. The camp operated until 1950. According to Hal Burton, formerly on the board of directors of the Mount Mansfield Ski Club, the cook at the Ranch Camp "always had a huge iron vat of good New England baked beans on the stove. It cost $2.50 a night, or free if you brought your own blankets. There were always a lot of very happy skiers inside. We felt privileged to have snow, because there weren't any snowmakers in those days." The camp used to be located near the junction of the current Burt Trail and the connector trail with the Ranch Valley Cruise.

The demise of the Ranch Camp occurred under unfortunate circumstances. In the late 1960s the buildings that composed the Ranch Camp were occupied by squatters—mostly young counterculture seekers who had fled the urban blight. The Burt Lumber Company, owners of the property, were unsure of how to handle the problem. They finally decided on a definitive solution. In September 1970 they burned down the buildings. There is now no trace left of the one-time forest enclave of Mount Mansfield skiers.

With the Ranch Camp as a base of operations in the thirties, a 3-mile climb up the Bruce Trail and a run back down was considered a pretty good day. But by 1937 the first commercial rope tow opened on the western slopes of the mountain above the Mount Mansfield Hotel, and by 1940 a 6,300-foot single chairlift opened (since replaced by the Forerunner Quad) capable of carrying two hundred skiers per hour up the mountain. The Bruce Trail on the undeveloped south side of the mountain was quickly abandoned in favor of the lift-served trails.

Local downhill skiers throughout the 1950s and 1960s occasionally skied the old CCC trails and kept them from becoming overgrown. Today, the Bruce Trail is cooperatively maintained by the Mount Mansfield and Trapp Family ski touring centers, and carrying on the proud heritage of these trails has largely been left to three-pin skiers. Together with the Teardrop Trail, the Bruce Trail endures as a crowning jewel in the CCC's network of down-mountain trails. A ski down the Bruce will make it clear why old-timers traveled so far for this prize.

The trail begins just behind the stone hut next to the Octagon. A sign for "South Link" marks the trailhead. The trail goes south, dropping straight down the fall line in a broad drainage. The trail is 15–20 feet wide, narrower than the Teardrop and about equivalent in steepness. The Bruce is full of quick corners and surprises. Fast reactions are needed. There is only one heart-stopping steep drop, the horizon line for which is clearly visible in advance. One man I spoke with who had skied the Bruce in its heyday during the thirties and forties said the technique of choice was to just "shuffle" down the trail. By frequently alternating the lead ski and letting it carve its own arc instead of trying to crank every turn, you can link a series of small S-turns all the way down. Try it—it still works and is a style well suited to this trail, particulary in powder conditions.

The Bruce is exposed to the southern sun. Because of this, it tends to have less consistent snow conditions than the Teardrop, which has northern and western exposures. It is common to encounter a wide range of snow types when skiing the Bruce, which adds to its interesting personality.

The Bruce Trail travels through some long, open birch glades before coming to a clearly marked intersection with the Overland Trail after 1.1 miles. Turning right here will lead to the Underhill Trail, just below the Needle's Eye (see the description in the Teardrop Trail section). If you have the time, climbing the Burt Trail to the Skytop ridge and skiing back to either the Trapp Family or the Mount Mansfield ski touring center makes a great day trip. The ski tour encompasses every type of skiing, from telemarking down a powder run, to backcountry touring, to double-poling or skating your way home on groomed trails.

The Bruce Trail continues straight ahead from its junction with the Overland Trail, ending a mile later at the Burt Trail. The Burt Trail is part of the Mount Mansfield Ski Touring Center. There are 1.2 miles of groomed trail skiing from the end of the Bruce to the touring center.

Mount Mansfield Region

Teardrop Trail

THE TOUR   The Teardrop Trail was another of the classic down-mountain trails cut in the 1930s by the CCC. It leaves just south of the Nose of Mount Mansfield and descends west off the buttress that forms the Forehead.

LENGTH   1.2 miles

ELEVATION   Bottom: 2,200 feet; top: 3,900 feet

MAPS   USGS Mount Mansfield (7.5-minute series, 1980); *Stowe Cross-Country Ski Map*, Northern Cartographic; GMC *Mount Mansfield Area* map

DIFFICULTY   Most difficult

HOW TO GET THERE   From the Mount Mansfield at Stowe ski area, take the Forerunner Quad Chairlift to the Octagon. The chairlifts can be used free of charge between 8 A.M. and 9 A.M. Ski or walk up the Toll Road to the summit, following it past some TV towers until the junction with the Long Trail South (sign). Ski on the Long Trail for 100 yards, passing the Forehead By-pass on the left. Continue bearing right for about another 100 yards to the remains of an orange trail sign (illegible). Teardrop Trail leaves to the right.

In 1937, encouraged by the instant renown that their ski trails on the Stowe side of Mount Mansfield had achieved, the Civilian Conservation Corps turned its energies to the "other

Telemarking in new powder on the Teardrop Trail.

side" of Mount Mansfield. Burlington-area skiers clamored for ski routes on Mansfield that didn't require driving all the way around to Stowe. So the Forest Service issued orders to the CCC to cut a trail that dropped from the summit of Mount Mansfield to the sleepy town of Underhill. Stowe's master trail engineer, Charlie Lord, was then serving on the technical staff of the CCC. He laid out the Teardrop Trail, and the CCC trail builders went to work. Perry Merrill gave the trail its name because, according to Lord, the trail was so fast "it made tears run from your eyes."

Underhill residents once had visions of a ski development on a par with that in Stowe. In the late 1930s, slopes were cut on the west side of Mount Mansfield. A 1,000-foot rope tow was installed, and the slopes were lighted for night skiing. Several intercollegiate ski meets were held on the slopes in the early 1940s, but the operation was abandoned after World War II.

The Teardrop was described in one account as "the pièce de résistance" of the trails in the Underhill area. A 1939 skiing guidebook proclaimed it as "one of the most thrilling trails in the East." It originally linked up with another trail and covered a total of 3 miles. A rope tow was at one time in operation at the base of it.

Despite this, the Teardrop never achieved the early popularity of the legendary Nose Dive, Chin Clip, and Bruce trails on the "front" side of the mountain. Early Stowe skiers such as Lord, Craig Burt, Jr., and the rest of their crowd simply felt it was too much of a hassle to have to climb up the mountain, ski down the Teardrop and then climb back up it again to return home. Downhill skiers from Underhill and Burlington used the trail and maintained it. Ironically, the Teardrop has probably achieved more renown today among Nordic skiers than it did in its early years.

So what's so special about an abandoned downhill trail like the Teardrop? Its loyal following would agree on at least one thing: powder. While weekend warriors are scraping their way down the icy slopes on the front side of the mountain, pinheads are floating through knee-deep fluff on the "back" side. The Teardrop is usually a reliable catchment area for powder even when the lowlands are starting to dry up.

Like many CCC ski trails, the Teardrop has unmistakable character. Turns were placed strategically in ways that kept the route interesting and challenging, and the trail takes advantage of special landscape features. But most important, the trail was located where the snow dumped most heavily and held longest—there were no snowmakers fifty years ago to replenish the trail after a day's ski.

Skiing the Teardrop still presents some logistical problems. Shuttling a car for the route is unwieldy. It is a 35-mile drive around Mount Mansfield to get from Stowe to Underhill. The usual solution is either to park at the bottom of the Teardrop and ski up it with skins, or to start at the Mount Mansfield at Stowe ski area, take the chairlift almost to the summit, ski the Teardrop and skin back up, and return to your car by skiing down one of the Mount Mansfield ski area trails. However, the most aesthetic option, described below, is to start from the Mount Mansfield at Stowe ski area and ski the Teardrop as part of an around-the-mountain ski tour.

The beginning of the Teardrop is deliberately difficult to find. Local skiers have left the start of the trail obscure in the hope of keeping skier traffic down. Despite these understandable efforts, the Teardrop is no longer a local secret. The fact that the word is out about the Teardrop, however, has not diminished its appeal. It is still wide and powdery enough to allow a number of skiers to make their own tracks.

The most difficult section of the Teardrop used to be at the top, where a narrow chute threaded among stunted trees before the trail opened up. Some overzealous trail work has changed this, and the upper quarter mile is now somewhat more easily negotiated, although it is usually windblown and icy. The trail quickly opens into a 30-foot wide swath heading due west. The trail slabs across the north side of a buttress that runs west from the Forehead. There is a slight double fall line to contend with for the first half of the run.

Back up the trail there is an impressive view of the cliffy western face of the Forehead. The trail soon begins its characteristic rock-and-roll style, with alternating steep drops and gradual run-outs—and barely enough time to catch your breath in between. Skiing the Teardrop evokes the same sensation as paddling a good white-water run: adrenaline surging as you brace through the big drops, moving slowly through a calm section while contemplating what's ahead, and being lured in, before you realize it, to the next chute.

The trail drops down quickly, and after 1 mile it intersects with the old CCC Road. The Teardrop then makes a jog of about 30 yards to the left, where it continues downhill for another 0.2 mile. This lower section (referred to as the "Lower Teardrop" on the *Stowe Cross-Country Ski Map*), starts with the steepest drop yet. The trail then darts through open forest, ending the run with some first-rate tree skiing. With this final section, the Teardrop covers a full range of downhill skiing terrain, from narrow chutes, to broad powder skiing, to tighter tree shots. You can pull out all the stops on this trail and try everything in your bag of tricks. This variety is what makes the route so interesting and rewarding to ski.

The Teardrop has developed something of a cult following among local skiers. It has gone from being a historical relic to become a trail where fierce races take place among skiers vying for first tracks after a storm. In good conditions, some people will come to ski the trail several times in a day, and then return the next day to ski it again. The passions that this route inspires are understandable; it may be the best powder run in New England when conditions are right.

As with all trails, the difficulty of the Teardrop is influenced by the snow conditions, which in turn are largely affected by the amount of skier traffic. On a good weekend, the Teardrop can easily have several dozen skiers tearing it up. Since the special character of the Teardrop is really that it is a powder run, the spirit of this trail just is not captured when there are moguls on it. Therefore, the best time to catch it is just after a storm, preferably midweek.

The Teardrop ends at the W.B. Trail. This junction is

marked only by orange plastic blazes and is easy to miss.
Turning right on the W.B. brings you back to the CCC Road
and the parking lot in Underhill State Park. Turning left will
lead uphill 2 miles on a sparsely blazed trail to the Underhill
Trail and the Needle's Eye. This presents the most interesting
way to ski the Teardrop; you can ski back all the way around
the mountain to finish at the Mount Mansfield Ski Touring
Center, which is just up the road from the Mount Mansfield
at Stowe ski area parking lot. The Needle's Eye is an impos-
ing-looking rock cleft that separates the long Mount Mansfield ridge from Dewey Mountain to the south. The ski trail
skirts the Needle's Eye by cutting right (south), passing
through a col known as the Devil's Dishpan. Just the other
side of this col, a trail junction is reached with the Overland
Trail, which connects with the lower section of the Bruce
Trail in 0.7 mile. The Overland drops quickly at first as it
descends a narrow drainage but soon flattens out as it approaches its junction with the Bruce Trail. Turning right
(east) on the Bruce leads to the Burt Trail, part of the trail
system of the Mount Mansfield Ski Touring Center. The Burt
Trail ends at the touring center on Mountain Road. The total
distance for this round-the-mountain tour is 5.3 miles. Leave
plenty of time in which to ski it because you will likely be
breaking trail for most of the way.

Mount Mansfield Region
Nebraska Notch Trail

THE TOUR   A ski tour from the Underhill side of Mount Mansfield into Nebraska Notch

LENGTH   2.9 miles from trailhead to Taylor Lodge

ELEVATION   Starting: 1,400 feet; high point: 2,000 feet

MAPS   USGS Mount Mansfield (7.5-minute series, 1980) and Bolton Mountain (7.5-minute series, 1948); *Stowe Cross-Country Ski Map*, Northern Cartographic; GMC *Mount Mansfield Area* map

DIFFICULTY   Moderate/more difficult

HOW TO GET THERE   From Underhill Center, drive 0.6 mile north and turn right on Stevensville Road, which you follow for 1.6 miles until the road turns sharply left at a sign for the Maple Leaf Farm. The parking turnout for the Underhill and Nebraska Notch trails is 50 feet straight ahead from where the road turns left. It is a 1.1-mile ski in on the road to the trailhead. Caution is advised if you drive in farther on this road. Do not block any driveways, and be certain you can get your car out without getting stuck.

Nebraska Notch is the east-west passage between Mount Clark and Dewey Mountain. It is an exceptionally pretty area, one of those gems you occasionally stumble across in your travels through the mountains that keeps drawing you

A skier passing through the craggy Nebraska Notch en route to Taylor Lodge.

back for years. At one time a road passed through the notch, allowing passage from Stevensville to Lake Mansfield. It was a rough winter road that was eventually abandoned, the only trace of it being the ski and hiking trail described here.

According to one local inn owner, "In most places, people cut roads up the valleys. But in Vermont, there was always some guy who had a girlfriend over the next ridge, so he cut a road over the top of the mountain." If that is the case, one lovelorn Vermonter's labor is now a plum for skiers. This ski tour is a perfect day trip, combining classic Vermont vistas with fun woods skiing.

From the parking turnout, ski in on the road for 1.1 miles to a summer hikers' parking lot (unplowed). A sign here pointing to the right indicates that it is 1.7 miles to Nebraska Notch. The trail forks after 0.2 mile at an unmarked junction; the Underhill Trail is the trail heading off left, while the Nebraska Notch trail leaves right. Both trails are marked with blue blazes. The Nebraska Notch Trail rises gently through open hardwoods. Just before reaching the notch, the trail passes through a long, open birch glade, which is an irresistible tree-skiing romp on the way down.

Nebraska Notch is a craggy cleft through the mountains which is strewn with large boulders. Beaver ponds have flooded out the trees that once grew here. The winter scene is one of lone, defoliated trees dancing wildly in the wind. The curling sinews of uprooted trees evoke images of the ancient bristlecone pines of the White Mountains in California. Huge boulders lie helter-skelter about the frozen meadow.

At the east end of the notch, there is a marked trail junction where the Clara Bow Trail leaves left and the Long Trail proceeds right for 0.4 mile to Taylor Lodge. The Clara Bow Trail, described as "rough" on the sign, is a rock-strewn drainage that is best avoided. The trail to the right climbs up and over a col and drops suddenly to the three-sided wooden shelter maintained by the Green Mountain Club. Taylor Lodge was constructed in 1978 and named for James P. Taylor, the founder of the Green Mountain Club. It is a beautiful and spacious shelter that includes a porch, picnic tables, a loft, and sleeping room for twenty. The picturesque setting and the easy access make the lodge an ideal destination for a ski camping trip. An abundance of good skiing begins right at the doorstep.

There is a view from the shelter of Lake Mansfield below and the Skytop ridge up to the northeast. The Lake Mansfield valley is the only glacial cirque in Vermont and has long attracted the attention of geologists. The lake itself is man-made, the dam having been built originally to enhance local fishing.

The descent from Taylor Lodge over the notch and back to the beaver meadows can be made on the trail or through the open trees. This sets the tone for the rest of the ride down: ski it as you see it. There is good open forest skiing for nearly the entire distance back to the summer hikers' parking lot. This is a delightful, moderate downhill run on which you can link turns at your own pace. This is a good place to discover for yourself why Vermont skiers will travel so far to "ski the trees."

Mount Mansfield Region

Skytop Trail

THE TOUR   A rolling ridge trail with excellent views of Mount Mansfield. It connects a number of ungroomed backcountry ski trails of the Trapp Family and Mount Mansfield ski touring centers.

LENGTH   Rob George Saddle to Dewey Saddle: 2.8 miles; accessed by trails from Trapp Family (2.5 miles), Mount Mansfield (3.5 miles), or Topnotch (2.3 miles) ski touring centers

ELEVATION   Starting: 2,000 feet; high point: 3,000 feet

MAPS   USGS Bolton Mountain (7.5-minute series, 1948); *Stowe Cross-Country Ski Map*, Northern Cartographic

DIFFICULTY   Moderate/more difficult

FEE   This ungroomed trail is part of the trail network of the Trapp Family Ski Touring Center. A trail ticket from the Trapp Family Ski Touring Center or any of the cooperating touring centers must be purchased.

HOW TO GET THERE   The Skytop Trail is accessed by trails from the Mount Mansfield, Topnotch, or Trapp Family ski touring centers.

The Skytop Trail is one of the prettiest ski tours in New England. The trail follows a 3-mile-long ridge that lies in the heart of the rugged Mount Mansfield region. Traveling along

Afternoon sun on the Skytop Trail.

the lee side of the ridge, it is common to find freshly deposited powder on Skytop while there may only be crusty snow in the valleys below. With its knolls, hollows, and high clearings, Skytop is a small, romantic world unto itself, a place to retreat to from the madding crowds below.

The Skytop Trail offers pristine forest skiing at a high elevation—an unusual and picturesque combination. This ski tour can serve cross-country skiers as a convenient introduction to the backcountry because of its proximity to the Stowe-area touring centers. Accessed by skiing through the trail network of either the Trapp Family, Mount Mansfield, or Topnotch touring centers, the route is easy to follow and is sure to make track skiers begin to wonder what has kept them from wandering *off-piste* (off-trail) all these years.

The Skytop Trail was cut by the Burt Lumber Company in the late 1930s. It was originally used by skiers who wanted to make a loop trip from the Ranch Camp to the Conway Trail (now the Burt Trail). Craig Burt, Sr., owner of the Burt Lumber Company, was an important force in the expansion of skiing in the Mount Mansfield area. He was known as the "father of Stowe skiing." Burt was an avid skier himself, although by the account of his son, Craig Burt, Jr., he was no expert. His son describes how his father used to go out rabbit hunting with 8-foot-long, double-grooved skis and one pole to brake with. "His idea of fun was to take his skis, one ski pole, and a shotgun and go out for a rabbit hunt," recalls Burt. "He would bushwhack around, but he seldom came home with a rabbit."

The elder Burt used his loggers to open up trails in areas where they had already put logging roads. He wanted to link up existing roads and trails to create a large network on which skiers could spend a full day touring. He was partly motivated by the fact that his sons were enthusiastic skiers. Burt was responsible for a number of other ski trails and related developments, such as the Ranch Camp skiers' lodge (see the Bruce Trail route description) and providing the logging roads on which the Bruce Trail begins.

When Johannes von Trapp began looking into the prospects for opening up a ski touring center in the Mount Mansfield valley in the 1960s, it occurred to him that the ski trails and logging roads that had been abandoned when the downhill ski area grew would be perfect for developing again. In the spring of 1969, he climbed up to the Skytop ridge and went in search of the old blazes. He found most of them, and even came across an old first aid cache in the Dewey Saddle. Von Trapp says that he tried to have the new Skytop Trail follow the old route as much as possible. He credits the high quality of the wilderness trails in today's Trapp Family network to the fact that Craig Burt, Sr., was so meticulous about the way he cut logging roads. Since the roads had to be negotiated by oxen or horses, they were generally leveled well and cut with a moderate grade.

The Skytop Trail can be reached from the Trapp Cabin by following the Cabin Trail a short distance to the Rob George Saddle. The saddle is a large clearing with views of all the surrounding peaks. The Skytop Trail leaves off to the left. The trail quickly enters the forest and begins to climb steadily. Make note of what lies downhill of the switchback turns if you plan to come back the same way. If there is a light snow cover, this section often has a number of drainage divots on it. After a mile of steep climbing, the trail turns sharply south and begins to contour until it reaches the long ridge line that gives the tour its character, as well as its name. There is a sign indicating a scenic vista at the beginning of the ridge, where there are views of the surrounding peaks.

The route continues on rolling ground at 2,700 feet along the north side of the ridge. You may be breaking trail through deep snow here. The trail meanders around small ridge knolls and snakes its way through white birches. The forested ridge refracts the southern light, throwing zebralike stripes across the snow and the forest floor. The feeling up here is quiet and magical. Moose, deer, and other animals prance around freely on the ridge, unaccustomed to seeing people.

About two-thirds of the way along the ridge you will come across a first aid cache. Farther along, a short spur leads up to Lightning Knoll, an exposed rocky knob on the western end of the ridge. The knoll offers a wide-open view of Mount Mansfield and Smugglers Notch to the north. Just beyond Lightning Knoll a caution sign ("!") on a tree alerts you to the fact that you are about to drop steeply into Dewey Saddle, a col that separates Dewey Mountain from the Skytop ridge. The saddle marks the end of the Skytop Trail and the start of the Burt Trail.

Skiing down the Burt Trail is an enjoyable run through a wide, open hardwood forest. The Burt Trail was formerly the Conway Trail, one of the down-mountain ski trails that fed into the Ranch Valley which was cut by Craig Burt, Sr. Skiers can opt to follow the trail, which switchbacks down a broad drainage, or simply choose one of numerous lines through the open forest. In good conditions, this can be a delightful introduction to eastern tree skiing.

Other options for returning to the Trapp Family Ski Touring Center include backtracking on the Skytop Trail, which ends with an enjoyable, wide downhill trail descending from the ridge to the Rob George Saddle, or making a loop trip by returning on the Underhill Trail, which is mostly flat for its 2.7-mile distance back to where it meets the Skytop Trail. For those returning to the Mount Mansfield Ski Touring Center, continue on the Burt Trail for its full length. The Burt leads back to the parking lot at the Mount Mansfield Ski Touring Center. All junctions are clearly marked with trail signs.

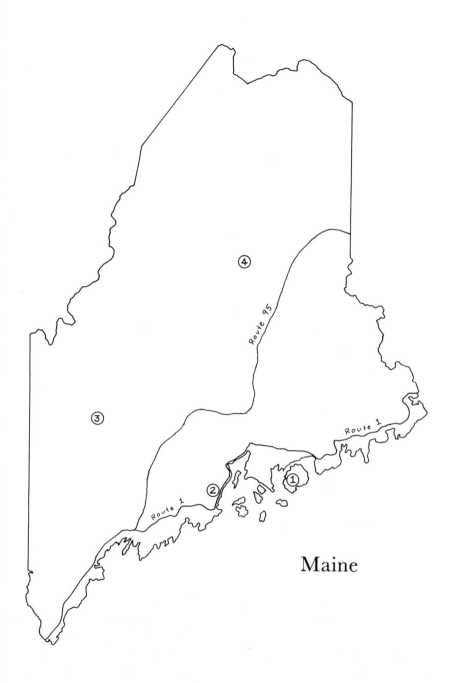

Route 95

Route 1

③

④

② ①

Route 1

Maine

Part IV

MAINE

1. Acadia National Park
2. Camden Hills State Park
3. Mount Blue State Park
4. Baxter State Park

A Note on Maps. In addition to the USGS and DeLorme maps that are referenced with each route, all of the routes described in this section are covered by maps that come with the *AMC Maine Mountain Guide,* 6th ed. The AMC maps can also be purchased separately. See the bibliography for additional information on maps.

Acadia National Park

THE TOUR   A scenic ski tour on Acadia's carriage roads and trails to the summit of Sargent Mountain, where there is excellent skiing on large snowfields overlooking the Atlantic Ocean

LENGTH   5.6-mile round-trip to Sargent Mountain summit, via direct route

ELEVATION   Starting: 400 feet; high point: 1,373 feet

MAPS   USGS Acadia National Park and Vicinity (1971); AMC Mount Desert Island map; DeLorme *Mount Desert Island–Acadia National Park Map*. Maps are for sale at park headquarters.

DIFFICULTY   Moderate

HOW TO GET THERE   From the north, follow ME 198 to the Parkman Mountain parking area, a half mile north of Upper Hadlock Pond. Park headquarters is just west of Eagle Lake on ME 233.

Acadia National Park offers some of the most unusual backcountry skiing in New England, if not in the country. The reason is the setting: Mount Desert Island sits in the Atlantic Ocean just off the coast of Maine. From the island's rocky, bare mountain summits, skiers have a 360-degree view of mile after mile of rugged Maine coastline and outlying islands and peninsulas. With the exception of the Olympic Mountains in Washington, no other mountain range in the continental

Skiing on the snowfields on Sargent Mountain over the Atlantic Ocean.

United States comes to mind that offers skiers the opportunity to ski high snowfields with an ocean backdrop. Here is a breathtaking setting for an afternoon of easy cross-country skiing, with enjoyable downhill skiing options.

Acadia is also special for the glimpse of cultural history that it offers. It was once a summer haven for blue-blooded eastern families such as the Fords, Carnegies, and Morgans—ME 3 leading into neighboring Bar Harbor was once known as "Millionaire's Row." The most popular ski routes in the park travel over paths originally laid to accommodate the horse-and-buggy ramblings of the Rockefellers and friends. Hiking the island's narrow foot trails was not John D. Rockefeller, Jr.'s idea of fun. So in 1917 he hired the noted landscape architect Frederick Law Olmsted, designer of New York's Central Park and Boston's "Emerald Necklace," to design and oversee construction of 51 miles of carriage roads. Rockefeller later donated most of these carriage roads to the federal government when Acadia National Park was created. They remain as a trademark of Acadia and are sought out by visitors to the area. No motorized transport, including snowmobiles, is allowed on the carriage roads.

Skiers in Acadia will appreciate what went into the construction of these paths. They are lined with shark's-tooth-shaped slabs of pink granite which were hand-cut. Turns and curves in the paths were designed to direct the attention of turn-of-the-century buggy passengers to particular scenic vistas. When drainages needed bridging, Rockefeller saw to it that they got no ordinary treatment. The sixteen bridges on the carriage roads, an attraction in themselves, were built with stones meticulously cut by local masons.

A classic ski tour in Acadia would naturally have to include a taste of all of these attractions, along with good skiing. Sargent Mountain fits the bill perfectly. Sargent is a 1,373-foot peak lying directly across from Cadillac Mountain (elevation 1,530 feet), the highest point on the East Coast. A carriage road that forms a horseshoe around the north slopes of Sargent goes higher (780 feet) than any other carriage road in the park. What few winter travelers have discovered is the

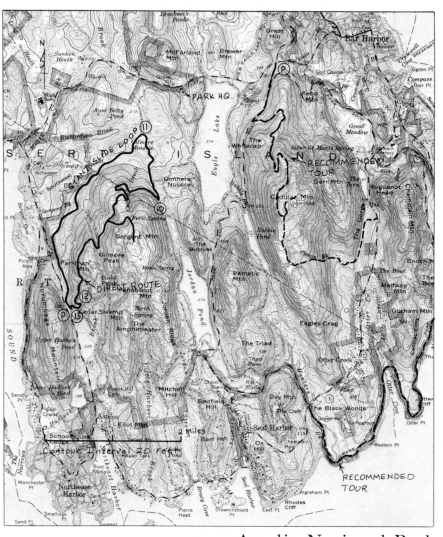

Acadia National Park

reward for leaving the carriage road to climb to the summit of Sargent. Skiers are in for a treat when they step off the beaten track here.

From the north side of the Parkman Mountain parking lot, turn right. Within 100 feet, you come to a junction with a carriage road. You may turn right here if you want the most direct route to Sargent Mountain (2.8 miles to the summit). Otherwise, a longer tour can be taken by turning left and skiing the Giant Slide Loop, which, when combined with a trip to the Sargent summit, is a 9.8-mile loop. Should you choose the latter route, you will ski for 3.2 miles on flat terrain before coming to carriage road junction 11, at which you turn right. You climb for 200 feet, cross six small bridges that span a wandering stream, and then make a sharp right at junction 10 onto a carriage road that climbs gently along the north face of Sargent Mountain. After 1.7 miles, the Sargent Mountain Trail leaves on the left, leading to the summit in 0.8 mile.

While skiing the carriage roads, note the intricate stonework that forms the borders of each path. It is also worth looking over your shoulder where the path turns in order to see what the original landscape architects were directing your attention to at each point. The path affords nice views to the west of Somes Sound, the only natural fjord on the eastern seaboard.

The trail up Sargent can be negotiated easily without climbing skins. Snow conditions after breaking out onto the summit slopes can be icy and somewhat treacherous. It will probably be easiest to carry your skis the short distance to the summit from treeline when this is the case. From the summit, the Atlantic Ocean glistens off to the south, the horizon broken only by occasional coastal islands. The windswept summit ridge tells the story of the glacier that shaped the landscape. Estimated at 2 miles in thickness, the ice cap slid over Acadia from the north, leaving deep north-south scratches in the rocks and grinding the island mountains into the characteristic domes that form the park's skyline. The lakes below were merely puddles that formed where the earth was scooped out by the ice cap as it made its way into the ocean.

Walking north along the summit ridge, you soon come to a series of snowfields that drop down the northwest slope of the mountain. These snowfields are hidden until you are practically on top of them. Depending on how much snow has fallen that year, you may link together a series of runs of several hundred feet each. These open slopes provide perfect moderate terrain for telemarking. It is easy to spend all afternoon exploring the skiing possibilities on the north slopes. But you can also spend as much time between runs just taking in the incredible panorama here.

Late in the season, when the prevailing winds deposit snow on the southern slopes of the mountain, there is good open skiing on the ridge going south from Sargent Mountain over Penobscot Mountain and down into the Amphitheater.

To return to your car from the summit of Sargent, drop back down the Sargent Mountain Trail and go left on the carriage road. There is not much of a downhill grade on the carriage roads, since they were designed to contour gently around the mountain. Go right at junctions 12 and 13; the Parkman Mountain parking lot will appear shortly on your left.

Snow conditions in Acadia are difficult to predict. The coastal climate may cause it to snow in Acadia when there has been little precipitation elsewhere in Maine, or it may rain here when snow has been dumped in the interior of the state. A call to park headquarters (207-288-3338) is helpful, but even the rangers tend to be overly pessimistic about the skiing possibilities. In mid-March, after rangers warned that I would be walking the whole route, I enjoyed a great day of skiing on Sargent. There is usually reliable snow in Acadia from Christmas through February. Good skiing continues on north-facing trails and slopes well into March, long after south-facing slopes have melted into rock and mud. The rule of thumb here is this: Don't wait—ski the snow when it falls. But lacking a recent storm, you are best off defying the pessimists and heading to the summits. The reward for playing the odds is that everyone else will have been discouraged by the official snow reports, saving all the great skiing on north-facing slopes for you.

Other Options. Cadillac Mountain offers good skiing on the auto road, which climbs 3.5 miles to the summit from a parking turnout on ME 233. The auto road is shared with snowmobilers, so trail conditions may be icy or choppy. During a good snow year, the snowfields and gullies on the east side of Cadillac just north of the Canon Brook Trail offer good open skiing.

The 51 miles of carriage roads are the most popular destinations for cross-country skiers in the park. The ski tour around Otter Point on the unplowed (sometimes plowed in one lane) Park Loop Road is exceptionally pretty where the road passes right alongside the ocean. The *Winter Activities Guide* available from park headquarters describes a number of other routes on the carriage and park roads.

Camden Hills State Park

THE TOURS   Coastal mountain skiing with panoramic views over the Penobscot Bay and Maine coastline

LENGTH   Ski Shelter Trail/Cameron Mountain Loop: 7 miles; Mount Battie Road: 2.8 miles round-trip to summit

ELEVATION   Starting: 250 feet; high point (Bald Rock Mountain): 1,101 feet

MAPS   The USGS Camden quadrangle (7.5-minute series, 1973) covers Mounts Megunticook and Battie; the USGS Lincolnville quadrangle (7.5-minute series, 1973) covers Cameron Mountain and Bald Rock. The AMC Camden Hills map covers the whole park. *Camden Hills State Park Trails System* is a sketch map listing trails and descriptions; it is available from the ranger. The USGS maps are available at the Village Shop or the Owl & Turtle Book Shop, both in Camden.

DIFFICULTY   Moderate

HOW TO GET THERE   To reach the Ski Shelter Trail trailhead, take US 1 north from Camden. Pass the ranger headquarters and the Mount Battie auto road entrance after 1.6 miles, and continue for another 4 miles to the junction of ME 173 north. Turn left on ME 173 and go 2.2 miles to Youngstown Road. This intersection is known as Stevens Corner. Turn left here; immediately on the left is the trailhead.

Telemarking on the summit of Bald Mountain overlooking Penobscot Bay.

The Camden Hills are a tightly grouped range of mountains clustered on the Atlantic coast just north of the town of Camden, Maine. Mount Megunticook (elevation 1,385 feet) in Camden Hills State Park is the highest point on the mainland coast of the eastern seaboard. (Cadillac Mountain in Acadia is the highest point on the east coast, but it is on an island.) For those who are torn between wanting to spend time near the sea and wanting to spend time in the mountains, the Camden Hills, like Acadia National Park to the north, constitute one of the few places where one can do both. As one Capt. John Smith wrote, Camden lies "under the high mountains of the Penobscot, against whose feet the sea doth beat." The experience you can have here of skiing high on a mountain snowfield with the ocean unfolding below you is an exhilarating one.

Skiers may be surprised to learn that the ubiquitous CCC trail builders made their presence felt all the way to Mount Megunticook. The current Slope Trail on the north side of Mount Megunticook is the approximate location of an old hand-graded CCC ski trail that was rated intermediate to expert. In its heyday, it was 30–60 feet wide. This trail was relocated in 1977 because of serious erosion problems. Virtually all trails in the park were used and rated for skiing throughout the 1930s. What the CCC eyed in the Camden Hills is still true today: it is an area that tends to accumulate good quantities of snow and has excellent terrain for skiing.

The summits of the Camden Hills are steeped in the history of the early wars that touched this area. Zeke's Lookout, a prominent viewpoint off the Zeke's Trail, was named for an old patriot who stood watch from this point in order to provide warning to the townspeople of enemy movement in Camden Harbor and Penobscot Bay during the War of 1812. Another person was paid twenty-five dollars to clear a rough road up Mount Battie in 1814 and to haul three cannons to the summit for the purpose of defending Camden from a naval attack.

Some of the best and most scenic skiing can be found on the northern side of the park. Both Bald Rock (elevation 1,101

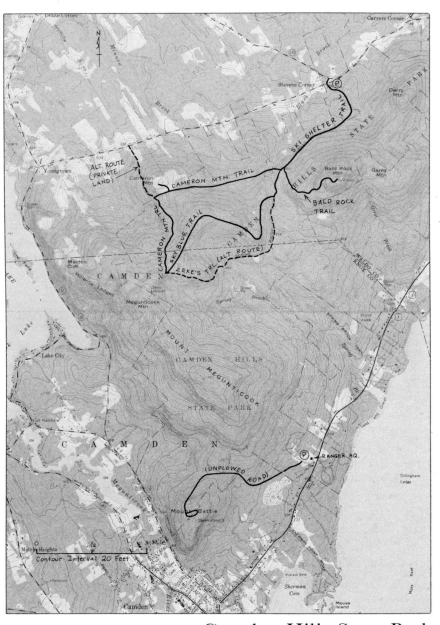

Camden Hills State Park

feet) and Cameron Mountain (elevation 811 feet) have exposed summits with views of Penobscot Bay. Both peaks are accessed via the Ski Shelter Trail.

The Ski Shelter Trail is an old fire road leading to a now abandoned ski shelter. The trail is now used by both snowmobilers and skiers in the winter. Ski up a gradual rise for 1.3 miles until you reach a gazebo and a four-way trail junction. Heading off left, it is 0.5 mile up the Bald Rock Trail to the summit, or turning right it is 1.1 miles to Cameron Mountain. The trail up Bald Rock climbs steadily but gradually through mixed forest. The trail is 10–12 feet wide, and with new snow it is an excellent moderate downhill run. From the cliffbound summit of Bald Rock, there is a panoramic view all the way to Cadillac Mountain in Acadia and a vista of the entire Camden Hills region. There is a small snowfield on the north side of the summit which can be skied.

The ski to Cameron Mountain is on flat terrain following an old town road and passing abandoned farmland. Cameron Mountain itself is a treeless blueberry knoll rising 100 feet above the ski trail. It serves as a fun, gentle telemarking hill, with a nice view to the northeast of the Penobscot Bay. Cameron Mountain is on private land, so skiers should inquire at park headquarters about permission to ski on it. From Cameron Mountain, you may continue briefly north on the trail to a junction. Bearing right at the junction will bring you back to Youngstown Road, where there is no official parking and no trail sign (utility pole 91 is the only marker). Bearing left, the Cameron Mountain Trail continues, climbing uphill to its junction with the Sky Blue Trail. This trail wanders downhill through open blueberry clearings and passes some huge old black spruce trees before meeting up again with the Ski Shelter Trail.

Another enjoyable ski tour in the park is up the unplowed road on Mount Battie (elevation 800 feet). From the parking lot behind the ranger's house, it is 1.4 miles uphill to the summit, and an enjoyable, sustained downhill ski back. The stone tower on the summit was erected in 1921 as a monument to the men and women who fought in World War I.

There is also a plaque honoring the poet Edna St. Vincent Millay, who drew inspiration for some of her most famous poems from her hikes in the Camden Hills. It is easy to understand why she was so struck by what she saw. From the summit, you are treated to a classic Maine vista of gentle, rounded hills, a patchwork of farm- and pastureland in the valleys, and the sea stretching off in the distance.

Other Options. A popular local skiing destination for those looking for flatter terrain is the Tanglewood area, located just north of Duck Trap. The area has a number of easy cross-country ski trails.

Mount Blue State Park

THE TOURS   A variety of trails through the rolling terrain of Mount Blue State Park, located in a wild, unspoiled area of Maine that is easily accessible

LENGTH   The ski trail loops are from 1.7 miles to 7 miles long, with longer variations if snowmobile trails are used.

ELEVATION   Starting: 1,100 feet; high point (Center Hill): 1,600 feet

MAPS   The USGS Dixfield quadrangle (15-minute series, 1956) covers the entire park; the USGS Weld quadrangle (7.5-minute series, 1968) covers the Center Hill area and most of the ski trails; and the USGS Mount Blue quadrangle (7.5-minute series, 1968) covers Mount Blue and the base area around it. The AMC Weld map covers the entire park. USGS maps are available at Towle's Hardware in Dixfield or Eagle's Sport Shop in Wilton.

DIFFICULTY   Moderate

HOW TO GET THERE   From I-95, take exit 12 (Auburn) to ME 4, following it to Wilton. Take ME 156 from Wilton to Weld. From Weld Village, take the road that leads uphill east from the four corners and bear left at the fork at 0.5 mile. Continue staight ahead to the ranger's house where there is a sign that says "snowmobile trails and parking." Snowmobile and ski trails begin here.

In the "wildest country": skiing in Mount Blue State Park, with Mount Blue in the background.

Maine is different from the other New England states. This difference was captured by Henry David Thoreau, who described it in his book *The Maine Woods* as simply "the wildest country." Much of Maine is relatively untamed. Until recently, parts of the state were not even definitively mapped. Unlike large tracts of Vermont and New Hampshire, which long ago embraced tourism and gentrification, Maine is still considered a backwater by the majority of weekend skiers. This is despite the fact that booming ski resorts like Sunday River in Bethel, Maine, are as close or closer to Boston than places like Sugarbush and Bolton Valley in Vermont, and just as worthwhile as a ski destination.

A trip to Mount Blue State Park offers a glimpse of this untamed side of New England. Despite its "out there" feeling, Mount Blue State Park is in fact only 40 minutes northeast of the Bethel area's two ski resorts and cross-country ski centers. A jaunt on the wild side up to Mount Blue would be a good way to round out a weekend ski trip to Sunday River or Mount Abrams.

When you turn off ME 2 and head north, the landscape slowly changes. Gone are the ubiquitous paper mills. Ski areas are nowhere in sight—only mile after mile of mountains, many inaccessible except by hiking or skiing a long way.

Mount Blue strikes a distinctive pose above the surrounding landscape. It is crowned by a perfectly shaped conical summit, glazed in white. It looks a bit comical, like a large ice cream cone sitting in the middle of the wilderness.

Mount Blue State Park is on 5,000 acres of land acquired by the state during the Depression era. This area was largely populated by small farmers, many of whom could not survive financially at the time. According to a local resident, "People just left with what they could carry on their backs and went to where they could feed themselves." The CCC arrived in the 1930s to develop the land that eventually became the state park. The log shelters at the picnic area near the top of Center Hill were typical CCC constructions.

There is excellent skiing in the park on the newly developed ski trails and on the snowmobile trails that crisscross the base

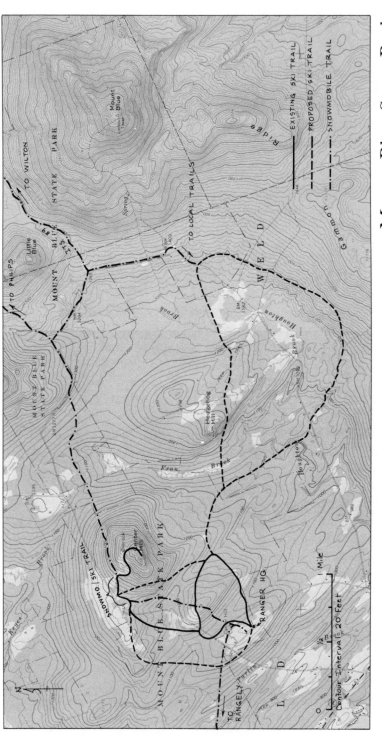

Mount Blue State Park

of Mount Blue. In 1987 rangers cut trails exclusively for cross-country skiers for the first time; by 1989 they hope to have as many as 12 miles of ski trails. The park has at least 10 miles of snowmobile trails and is the starting point of a 55-mile snowmobile trail that goes all the way to Rangeley.

Part of the reason that ski trails have not been developed until recently is simple: this part of New England is pickup truck and Ski-Doo country. Nobody's ever given much thought to providing for the lycra tights skiing crowd. The "snomo" users, as they're called, go to great pains to groom and maintain their trails. These trails make excellent wide paths for fast skiing and backcountry skating.

The highlight of the trail system here is a trip up Center Hill (elevation 1,658 feet). The ski trail intersects the unplowed auto road that ascends the hill up to the picnic area. The route to the summit continues to the top on the "scenic trail." The peak rises 300 feet above the unstaffed ranger cabin at the base of the hill. From the cleared summit, there are views of Jackson Mountain and Little Jackson Mountain, with their impressive snowfields. On a clear day you can see all the way to Old Speck in the Mahoosucs and to the White Mountains of New Hampshire to the southwest. The road makes a nice descent too. Check with the rangers to find out about the details of their newest ski trails.

The opportunity to explore Mount Blue State Park should be obvious to adventurous skiers. There is good skiing potential in the open glades on the Gammon Ridge, which runs southwest off the flanks of Mount Blue, as well as on the numerous logging roads in the valleys. Mount Blue itself is not particularly hospitable to ski. It has a narrow, steep snowmobile/hiking trail from the summit that requires some desperate survival skiing tactics. When I skied it with a friend, we affectionately nicknamed it "Mount Black and Blue."

Baxter State Park

THE TOURS   Ski mountaineering routes in the Chimney Pond region and ski touring in the Russell Pond area are two of the classic ski tours in the park. A north-south traverse of the park is also possible.

LENGTH   Golden Road/Compass Pond (parking) to Roaring Brook: 10.2 miles; Roaring Brook to Chimney Pond: 3.3 miles; Roaring Brook to Russell Pond: 7 miles

ELEVATION   Starting (Compass Pond): 530 feet; Chimney Pond: 3,000 feet; Russell Pond: 1,400 feet

MAPS   The USGS Katahdin quadrangle (15-minute series, 1949) covers Togue Pond to Russell Pond; the USGS Traveler Mountain quadrangle (15-minute series, 1955) covers Wassataquoik Lake to Grand Lake Matagamon; the AMC map of Katahdin and Baxter State Park and the DeLorme *Baxter State Park and Katahdin Map and Guide* cover the whole park.

DIFFICULTY   Chimney Pond: most difficult; Russell Pond: more difficult

FEE   Baxter State Park charges nightly fees for staying in lean-tos or bunkhouses and for camping within the park. Check with the park headquarters (207-723-5140) for current fees.

HOW TO GET THERE   Follow I-95 north to the Medway exit, then head west on ME 157 to Millinocket. Follow signs to the park. It is 14 miles from Millinocket to a small plowed parking area on the south side of the Golden Road just southeast of Compass and River ponds.

Baxter Peak on Katahdin, seen from Chimney Pond.
Photograph by Jeff Kuller.

Baxter State Park is home to some forty-six mountain peaks, eighteen of them over 3,500 feet. Encompassing more than 200,000 acres of protected land, the park is one of the largest single tracts of wilderness in New England. Baxter is arguably home to the best wilderness skiing in the East through its numerous mountains, valleys, and lakes. It is unmatched in the region for its potential as a destination for extended ski expeditioning.

Katahdin dominates the surrounding landscape of the park. At 5,267 feet, it is the highest point in Maine. Katahdin, whose name means "greatest mountain," is striking and unusual for a New England peak. The serrated ridges and the long, sweeping gullies that run off its summit remind one more of a western mountain than an eastern one. Its massive size is at the same time awe-inspiring and intimidating. The summit ridge is part of a 4-mile-long plateau that rises 4,500 feet above the surrounding lowlands to the south. This tableland is bounded by a number of impressive glacial cirques, or basins.

At least as impressive as the size of the park is the fact that so large a place exists in Maine that isn't being relentlessly logged. This distinction was hard won by the defenders of the park, and it took a former governor of Maine, Percival Proctor Baxter, to make it happen. Baxter, a Portland native, was a frequent visitor to the north country. He was determined to preserve the area around Katahdin as a park, but this wish pitted him against the "shadow government" of Maine: the large lumber interests. Despite being known to hikers for its beauty, the park was better known to loggers as prime timber country. The lumber companies made it known that they would only leave if they were bought out at a good price.

Baxter decided to raise money and buy the land himself. It took him forty-five years of fund-raising from private interests and working to pass legislation before his dream was realized. Today Baxter State Park is protected by the former governor's covenant that declared that the land in the park would "forever be left in its natural wild state, forever be kept as a sanctuary for wild beasts and birds, and forever be used for

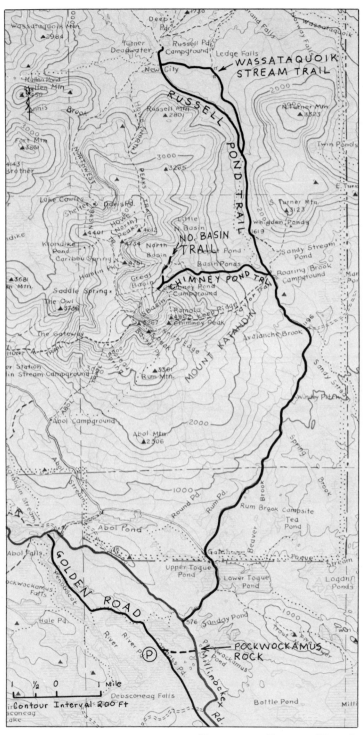

Baxter State Park

public forest, public park, and public recreational purposes." Indian legends of Katahdin and stories about the geology of the park, as well as useful trail information, are included in the DeLorme *Baxter State Park and Katahdin Map and Guide.*

First-time winter visitors to Katahdin may be surprised to find themselves confronting one of its most difficult obstacles before they even leave their homes: the Baxter State Park bureaucracy. Baxter has notorious rules and regulations that govern entry into the park in winter, defined as the period from December 1 to April 1. This includes applying at least two weeks in advance of arriving for a special use permit (which can be denied) for camping or climbing, designating a "trip leader" and alternate leader for whom outdoor resumés must be submitted, requiring a minimum of four people per party, providing a day-by-day itinerary of where you intend to stay, signing in and out with a ranger if you plan to travel above timberline, and finally, getting your equipment and party checked out by park rangers at the park entrance. Only after all these conditions have been met may you head off into the solitude of the park. But it is not over yet. If you are staying at Chimney Pond, you must wait until 7:00 A.M. each morning when the ranger determines whether Katahdin itself will be "open" or "closed," depending on weather conditions.

Mountaineers have long considered the rules and regulations of Baxter an affront to the ethic of self-reliance that most wilderness travelers embrace. Guy and Laura Waterman, writing in *Off Belay* in 1977, charged that the rules "stifle the 'freedom of the hills' so successfully that many climbers simply avoid Katahdin rather than submit." Park authorities explain themselves in their literature, saying that the purpose of the regulations is "to promote safety of all persons using the Park and to protect the Baxter State Park Authority and its staff from unnecessary search and rescue efforts." These rules actually represent a relaxation of past practices, when every party member had to submit a physical exam form signed by a doctor.

The rules and regulations for Baxter may change somewhat from year to year. Suffice it to say that a trip to the park must be planned at least one month in advance. If you are even considering a trip to Baxter, contact the Baxter State Park Authority, 64 Balsam Drive, Millinocket, ME 04462 (207-723-5140), well in advance and request their literature and applications for winter use. If you plan to ski in any of the basins (that is, above treeline), this is considered technical "alpine skiing" and you must apply for a special permit and provide additional information in your application.

Skier Dick Hall says a first visit to Katahdin is "like going to Disneyland"—you just ski around checking out the views and size of the mountain but don't really plan to accomplish much. There is something to say for this approach. Visitors to the park in winter need not set an ambitious itinerary. It is enough to come to look and take in the grandeur of the place. The bunkhouses, with their bay window views of the summits, are a comfortable base from which to take day trips. Two areas of major interest to skiers are the Chimney Pond area and the Russell Pond area. The Chimney Pond region is the traditional destination for winter climbing in the park. It lies at the foot of Katahdin in the heart of the Great Basin. Skiers can make reservations to stay at the bunkhouse, to camp in a lean-to, or to pitch a tent, all next to Chimney Pond.

Most of the ski routes from Chimney Pond require a high degree of both skiing and mountaineering skill. Skiers are warned that the most extreme avalanche hazard in the eastern Undited States exists on the slopes and in the gullies of the Great Basin. Snow instability is typically highest early in the season, from January through early March. At least one member of your party should be experienced in avalanche hazard evaluation, and all skiers planning to ski in any of the basins should carry avalanche rescue equipment, including shovels and rescue transceivers ("peepers"). *Avalanches on Katahdin are common*—choose your routes with extreme caution!

Skiing in to Chimney Pond from the Roaring Brook campground is strenuous. The Chimney Pond Trail climbs 1,400 feet in 3.3 miles. Most people are carrying in food and gear for a week, which compounds the effort required. Parties gen-

erally allot a day and a half to two days for skiing in to either
Chimney Pond or Russell Pond, and a day to ski out. This
partly explains why winter trips to the park are usually at
least a week long.

The reward for the trip to Chimney Pond is the humbling
view of South Basin. For skiers looking to "ski the steeps," this
is the place. South Basin has been described as having the
skiing qualities of "a hundred Tuckerman Ravines." It is a
north-facing glacial cirque that wraps like a horseshoe around
the southern side of Chimney Pond. Large snowfields drop
from the upper cliffs of the Cathedral Buttress on the west
side of the ravine, and on a clear day it is possible to see
almost to the summit of Baxter Peak.

There is challenging skiing on slopes of 30 degrees and
greater on the walls that flank the ravine. You can ski up to
the base of the gullies that begin in the basin, going as high as
you feel comfortable, and skiing down. One of the nicer routes
of this nature ascends Chimney Pond Brook (the drainage
running south out of the pond) up toward the base of the
Chimney, a prominent gully in the center of the ravine.

For a more moderate ski tour from Chimney Pond, a day
trip from the campground over to North Basin is a beautiful
traverse that links the two most impressive basins near the
mountain. North Basin is not visited frequently, especially in
winter. It is a wild, remote place, with spectacular walls and
gullies that rise 1,500 feet to the summit of the Howe Peaks.
The northern wall is a huge cliff.

The route to North Basin from Chimney Pond follows the
North Basin Trail. It is 1.4 miles to the floor of North Basin.
The North Basin Trail leaves the trail to Basin Ponds 0.3 mile
from Chimney Pond. The trail climbs through a spruce forest
and soon passes around the lower buttress of the Hamlin
Ridge, passing a junction with the Hamlin Ridge Trail. The
trail is moderately graded but can be rocky in light snow
cover. The trail then passes the lip of North Basin and climbs
up Blueberry Knoll. Blueberry Knoll is a spectacular vantage
point from which there are views into both North Basin and
South Basin. The North Basin Trail ends here, but it is possi-

ble to bushwhack another 0.2 mile to the floor of North Basin where there are two small ponds. You can ski around the floor of the ravine right up to the cliffs.

The Russell Pond area is a ski adventure with a different quality than that of a trip to Chimney Pond. Russell Pond is a peaceful crossroads in the midst of a vast, upheaved landscape. The pond lies in a pockmarked valley dotted with numerous lakes, all of them linked by small brooks. A trip to this area is a first-class wilderness ski tour. The terrain is gentle throughout the area.

From Roaring Brook Campground, skiers take the Russell Pond Trail. It crosses the Wassataquoik Stream and its drainages a number of times in the first 4 miles from Roaring Brook. At 3.3 miles the Wassataquoik Stream Trail (listed on some older maps as the Tracy Horse Trail) diverges to the right. The Wassataquoik Stream Trail was recently reopened, and it travels over flatter terrain than does the Russell Pond Trail in this section. It follows an old tote road and passes two lean-tos 5.6 miles after Roaring Brook. Camping is permitted at the shelters. The trip to the Russell Pond Campground is 7 miles via the Russell Pond Trail and 7.6 miles via the Wassataquoik Stream Trail.

Russell Pond is the gateway to the northern peaks in the park. From the pond there are views south to Katahdin and north to Traveler Mountain and Pogy Mountain. It is an exceptionally pretty area. Wildlife is abundant here; sightings of moose, pine marten, and other animals are common. Russell Pond Campground has a bunkhouse and lean-tos. Reservations are required for both. From the Russell Pond area, day trips can be made to the many lakes that lie to the west, or east to the interesting old remains of logging activity.

Despite the moderate skiing on a trip to Russell Pond, skiers must still consider a winter ski trip anywhere in the park to be a serious undertaking. Severe weather can set in for days, making travel to all areas impossible. Extra food should be brought in anticipation of such unpredictable events.

There are many other possible ski tours in Baxter State Park. An ambitious north-to-south hut-to-hut tour can be started just south of the Matagamon gatehouse. The perimeter road is plowed up to the Dudley Matagamon Wilderness Campground, which is just east of the bridge that crosses the East Branch of the Penobscot River. From there, the route goes 4.1 miles along the unplowed perimeter road to the newly constructed bunkhouse at Trout Brook Farm. The route continues 7 miles to the South Branch Pond bunkhouse, and another 9.6 miles to the Russell Pond bunkhouse. It is 7 miles from Russell Pond to the last bunkhouse at Roaring Brook, and a 10.2-mile trip out to the Golden Road from there. It is possible (for a fee) to arrange a car shuttle to Matagamon with a local person in Millinocket; inquire at the park for suggestions on whom to contact.

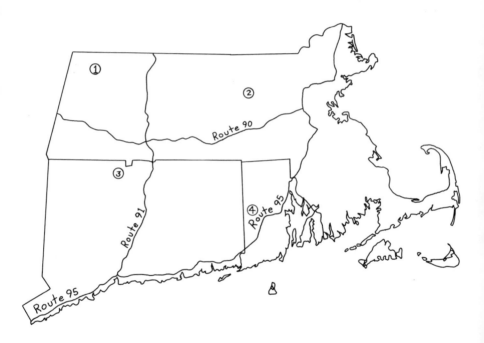

Southern New England

Part V

SOUTHERN NEW ENGLAND

1. Mount Greylock, Massachusetts
2. Wachusett Mountain, Massachusetts
3. Pine Mountain, Connecticut
4. Arcadia Management Area, Rhode Island

A Note on Maps. Recent-issue USGS 7.5-minute maps cover all of the tours in this section. An excellent collection of maps for Massachusetts skiers is the *Western Massachusetts Trail Map Pack,* available from New England Cartographics. It includes up-to-date maps of Mount Greylock, Wachusett Mountain, Mount Tom, Mount Toby, and a number of state parks, with ski trails highlighted. See the bibliography for additional information on maps.

Massachusetts

Mount Greylock

THE TOUR   The Thunderbolt Trail was one of the most famous ski race courses of the thirties and forties. It drops 1,700 vertical feet in 1.6 miles, beginning just below the summit. It ends at Thiel Farm in Adams.

LENGTH   Thunderbolt Trail (Thiel Farm to Appalachian Trail): 1.6 miles; Bellows Pipe Trail to Upper Thunderbolt, round-trip: 7.2 miles

ELEVATION   Start (Thiel Farm): 1,300 feet; high point: 3,100 feet

MAPS   USGS Williamstown, Massachusetts-Vermont (7.5-minute series, 1973). The most up-to-date map is the Mount Greylock map published by New England Cartographics. Sketch maps of trails are available from the Mount Greylock Visitor Center in Lanesborough and Western Gateway Heritage State Park in North Adams.

DIFFICULTY   Most difficult

HOW TO GET THERE   *To Thunderbolt trailhead in Adams:* Drive up Maple Street west from the McKinley Monument on MA 8 in the center of Adams. At the end of Maple Street, turn left onto West Road for 0.4 mile, pass a "crossroad" sign, and turn right on Gould Road (paved, no sign). Bear right at a fork on Thiel Road and park where plowing ends. Ski in 0.75 mile to the old Thiel Farm and the bottom of the Thunderbolt. *To Bellows Pipe trailhead:* From MA 2

Descending the Appalachian Trail en route to the Thunderbolt, just below the summit of Mount Greylock.

just west of North Adams center, take Notch Road (entrance opposite Mobil station and cemetery), bearing left after 2.1 miles at a T-intersection, and follow it to a 90-degree corner where plowing ends. Notch Road (unplowed, snowmobile route) leaves sharply right, and the Bellows Pipe Trail goes straight ahead (south).

The Thunderbolt. The intimidating name brings a smile to the face of older skiers. It is described in sobering terms in a 1939 guidebook to eastern skiing as "one of the steepest and most difficult expert trails in the East." The ski trail up Massachusetts' highest mountain (elevation 3,491 feet) was designed by Charlie Parker, a former caretaker of Bascom Lodge and avid skier. This lodge on the summit of Mount Greylock is now operated by the Appalachian Mountain Club and is open from April through October. The CCC provided the muscle to turn Parker's idea into reality.

Once it was built in the early 1930s, the Thunderbolt quickly attracted a loyal following among New England skiers. It was one of a small number of Class A ski racing trails (trails with a vertical drop of about 2,000 feet within a specified distance) in the Northeast, and as such it became the scene of numerous national and regional championship races. As a Class A trail, it was one of the places where ambitious racers could earn a coveted rating: skiing the Thunderbolt in less than 3 minutes made one an "A" racer, between 3 and 4 minutes qualified one as a "B" racer, and a "C" rating went to those who could schuss it in 4–6 minutes. The record time on the Thunderbolt was 2 minutes, 19.4 seconds, set by Bob Livermore in the 1940 U.S. Eastern championship race.

A virtual skiing subculture thrived around the Thunderbolt. A number of ski clubs, including the Mount Greylock Ski Club, the Thunderbolt Ski Club, and the Ski Runners of Adams, as well as local college teams from Williams and Amherst colleges, made the pilgrimage to the summit of Greylock every weekend. According to people who were regu-

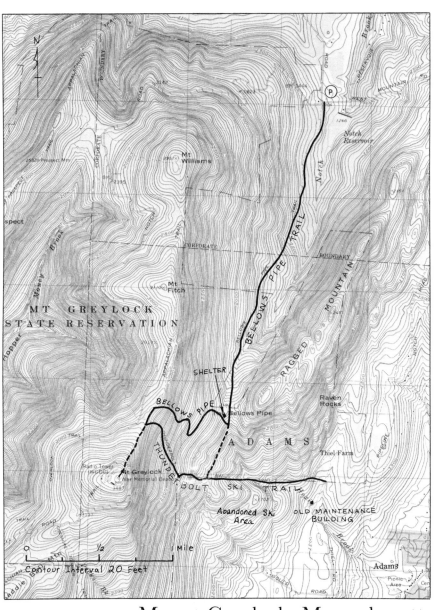

Mount Greylock, Massachusetts

lars on the trail in the 1930s, a typical weekend crowd on the Thunderbolt would average between thirty-five and forty skiers, with more on weekends preceding a big race. Skiers would sidestep up the trail, packing the snow on the big turns so it wouldn't get scraped off, and "filling the bathtubs" of skiers who fell. Spectators at the races would usually take part in the trail packing too.

The original Thunderbolt race trail started from the summit of Mount Greylock and traveled down what is now the Appalachian Trail a short distance before banking east onto what is now considered the beginning of the trail. Running parallel to the Thunderbolt was the Bellows Pipe Trail (sometimes referred to as the Bellows Pipeline), which was considered an intermediate trail. The upper section of the Bellows Pipe still exists, but the easy trail that today runs southeast from Notch Road to where it turns sharply uphill past a lean-to (now called the Bellows Pipe) was not part of the original trail. The lower section of the Bellows Pipe ran parallel to the Thunderbolt for its entire length and is now abandoned.

Skiers of today can test their talents on the Thunderbolt and get a humbling taste of what the old-timers were pioneering fifty years ago. Don't expect a geriatric meander, though: this trail is for skiers who like a lot of vertical drop in a short distance. It is an exhilarating steep run that will keep you swooping through turns throughout its entire length.

A potentially promising recent development that will affect the Thunderbolt is the new Heritage Greylock recreation resort being developed on the east side of Mount Greylock. The state and a private developer have joined forces to create an ambitious Nordic skiing center that includes the old Thiel Farm property at the foot of the Thunderbolt. The current plans include restoring the Thunderbolt and Bellows Pipe to their original state as down-mountain ski trails.

To get to the bottom of the trail from the junction of Thiel Road and Gould Road, ski on the unplowed Thiel Road for 0.6 mile past an old maintenance building. This building was to be part of a ski area that was never completed. Just past the building a growth of young evergreens marks the former Thiel Farm. The Thiel Farm was the site of the skiers' parking lot in the early days of the trail. Turn sharply left just north of the evergreens and watch for the trail entering the woods about 20 feet south of a large boulder. The trail climbs steeply, passing a cutoff at 0.8 mile where an old access road heads north to connect with the Bellows Pipe Trail in 0.3 mile.

In order to access the Thunderbolt from the Bellows Pipe Trail, follow the latter as it climbs gradually until you reach a junction (2.6 miles) marked by orange flashing. The trail turns sharply right (northwest) here, passes a lean-to, and climbs steeply up seven switchbacks. Several abandoned trails leave south to connect with the Thunderbolt, but the Bellows Pipe continues up until it meets the Appalachian Trail (AT). The sign marking the start of the Thunderbolt is on the AT 0.1 mile south of the Bellows Pipe–AT junction. For those interested in retracing the entire original route of the Thunderbolt, the summit of the mountain (along with a large war memorial tower, the AMC lodge, and a paved road) is 0.4 mile beyond this junction.

Bob Linscott, 1942 state champion on the Thunderbolt, recalls that the run from the summit began with a bang. Dropping from the parking lot, he recounts, the trail quickly crossed Rockwell Road and then dropped off precipitously as it headed for the junction where it bears east. "You would come off that road and be in the air for 50 feet—and that was if you weren't trying to get air. If you jumped, you'd go a lot further," he recalls.

Arriving at the Thunderbolt from the summit without having skied up it is exciting in its own right. A nondescript spur leaves the AT, and just 50 yards beyond, the whole side of the mountain drops away, revealing unobstructed views of the Berkshires and the southern peaks of the Green Mountains. Lying before you is the impressive beginning of the Thunderbolt.

The legions of skiers who lived to ski the Thunderbolt had names for every turn and dip on it; that was part of its personality. What is now the start of the trail at the AT was called the Big Turn, because it was the first committing turn after the straightaway descent from the summit. The trail then hits the Big Bend, where it turns sharply and steeply east. After a long southerly traverse where the trail drops over two to three ledge steps (these can be icy), the trail enters what is still described respectfully as the Needle's Eye. This is the crux of the Thunderbolt. The trail narrows here and turns to the left, although the slope banks downhill into the woods. "If a skier came down and hit the Needle's Eye full tilt and didn't make the turn, he was in deep trouble," muses Linscott. Just beyond the Needle's Eye is the Big Schuss, the steepest drop on the trail. At one time a rope tow was operated on the Big Schuss; the snatch block for it can still be seen high up in a tree at the top of the slope.

At the bottom of the Big Schuss (0.75 mile from the AT), a somewhat obscure connector trail leaves to the left. This leads back to the Bellows Pipe and should be taken by those making a loop trip back to Notch Road. This connecting trail was once known as the Apple Tree Trail because of a large apple tree that stood in the center of the path. Descending the Bellows Pipe back to Notch Road, be alert for numerous drainage divots on the trail, some of which may be open.

The lower section of the Thunderbolt continues to the right at the bottom of the Big Schuss (there is a sign on a large birch tree). From here to the finish line, ski racers of the past still had to contend with the Bumps, so named for the eight to ten large bumps that had to be negotiated, head into the "S" Turn, and ski the Last Drop, the final steep pitch, before crossing the brook to the finish line.

To Linscott, who was sixteen years old when he won the championship, the memory of skiing the Thunderbolt is still fresh. "By the time you hit the S Turn, your legs are gone and your wobbly knees are bumping up and down. . . . You were awfully glad to see the finish line when it came. Most skiers could just about stand up at the end."

The Thunderbolt today is 20–40 feet wide, with open woods on either side. It is a telemark playground in good conditions. The route is rarely skied anymore, but it is apparent that some local devotees of the trail maintain it and brush out much of the overgrowth. Given its light usage, chances of claiming first tracks on this route are good, and there is plenty to ski even if others have gotten to it before you. You're also bound to gain some new respect for your elders after making it down.

Other Options. There is a network of cross-country ski trails from the Mount Greylock Reservation Visitor Center in Lanesborough. Another good downhill ski option is to descend the Bellows Pipe from its junction with the AT. It was originally cut as an intermediate downhill ski trail. People looking for a less demanding route would enjoy the lower section of the modern-day Bellows Pipe, which offers easy cross-country skiing through gentle terrain. The Notch Road, used by snowmobilers, is a long, gentle downhill for those wishing to ski to the summit and back, but it often gets icy due to the heavy snowmobile use.

Another excellent backcountry ski tour in the area is the Taconic Crest Trail. It is a beautiful 26-mile traverse along the crest of the Taconic Range on the Massachusetts–New York border. The trail begins in North Pownal, Vermont, and runs south to Hancock, Massachusetts, where it joins the Taconic Skyline Trail. Trail descriptions can be found in the *AMC Massachusetts and Rhode Island Trail Guide* and the ATC *Guide to the Appalachian Trail in Massachusetts-Connecticut.*

Wachusett Mountain

THE TOURS   The Pine Hill Trail was a popular downhill ski trail on the east side of the mountain in the 1930s. Administration Road is a pleasant run from the summit of the mountain.

LENGTH   Pine Hill Trail: 0.5 mile to summit; Administration Road to Summit Road to summit: 1.75 miles

ELEVATION   Starting: 1,350 feet; high point: 2,006 feet

MAPS   USGS Wachusett Mountain, Massachusetts (7.5-minute series, 1972). The *Mount Wachusett State Reservation Trail Map,* free from the park visitor center, is a good topographic trail map. A better map, which includes a topographic map of Leominster State Forest on the back, is available from New England Cartographics.

DIFFICULTY   Pine Hill Trail: most difficult; Administration Road: moderate

HOW TO GET THERE   From MA 2, go south on MA 140 for 3 miles. Turn right on Mile High Road and pass the downhill ski area parking lots. The headquarters for the Mount Wachusett State Reservation is on the right. The John H. Hitchcock Visitor Center is open from 8:00 A.M. to 4:00 P.M. Note that the gate to the parking lot is locked at 4:00 P.M., so you will want to check with the ranger if you plan to be returning after that time.

To reach Administration Road, drive south past the visitor center and make the first right, which is Westminster Road. Administration Road leaves to the north, 2.4 miles beyond the visitor center.

Heading up Administration Road to the summit of Wachusett Mountain, overlooking central Massachusetts.

Wachusett Mountain (elevation 2,006 feet) is the highest peak east of the Connecticut River in Massachusetts, and it dominates the skyline of the central part of the state. It overlooks surrounding woodlands and is home to a thriving downhill ski area on its northern slopes. Being just over an hour away from Boston, it tends to get a good deal of hiker and skier traffic.

As was the case on many New England mountains, the steep flanks of Wachusett Mountain did not deter local farmers. The mountain was burned by Indians to improve hunting and cleared by farmers for agriculture in the early nineteenth century. The stone walls that crisscross the sides of the mountain are testimony to the determination of early farmers to utilize all the land they could in order to earn a living. It was not until just before the turn of the century, when many farmers abandoned the land in favor of industrial work in New England, that the mountain was first used for recreational purposes. A summit house was erected in 1884, symbolizing the changing view of the mountain, from that of needing it just for a livelihood to using it for recreation.

Wachusett was yet another target for the energetic CCC ski trail cutters. The Pine Hill Trail was a Class A racing trail designed about 1933 by Charles Proctor and built by the CCC. It was the site of the Massachusetts State Downhill Championships during the 1950s. On a typical weekend in the thirties and forties, there would be fifty to seventy-five skiers a day on the trail. Its primary use was recreational, but it was also a popular site for ski club races. Use of the trail declined in the early 1960s when a T-bar was installed on the north side of the mountain. The T-bar was replaced by chairlifts in the 1980s. It was, and still remains, the steepest trail on Wachusett Mountain, with a maximum grade of 25 degrees.

The Pine Hill Trail is now unofficially and sporadically maintained by a group of older skiers who live nearby. Once as wide as 45 feet, the trail has grown in so that it is now about half its original width. It presents a challenge to the best skiers.

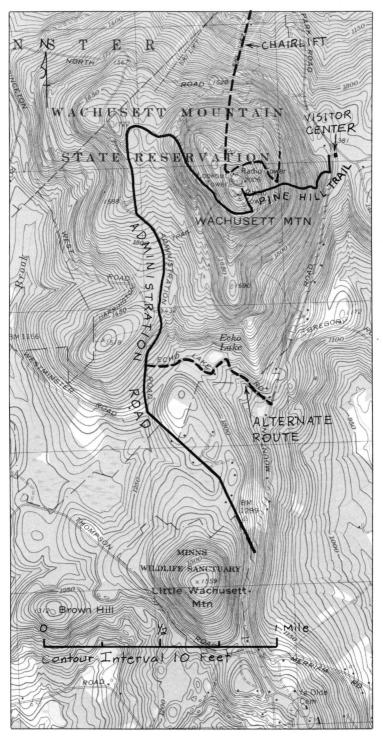

Wachusett Mountain, Massachusetts

The Pine Hill Trail leaves the Bicentennial Trail 0.2 mile from the parking lot. Only 0.5 mile long, it climbs 550 feet in a straight line to the summit. It is the shortest route from the visitor center to the top of the mountain. The trail is broken 0.1 mile from the summit by the "Down" Summit Road, which becomes part of the network of ski area trails just 50 feet north of where the Pine Hill Trail crosses it.

A number of options for creating loop tours exists. Taking the Loop, Mountain House, and Link trails to the summit and descending on the Pine Hill Trail is one good way of skiing a circuit. All of the trails on Wachusett tend to be rocky and require a fair amount of snow cover to fill in adequately.

The summit of Wachusett gets mixed reviews aesthetically. Though the views over eastern Masschusetts are excellent, Wachusett is one of those unfortunate New England peaks that has been thoroughly desecrated, in this case by three radio towers, a fire tower, chairlift stations, and a road. It is not exactly a wilderness environment. Wachusett once had a summit hotel, but it burned down. It has always puzzled me why New Englanders have had such a penchant for chopping roads up their most beautiful mountains and then constructing summit hotels. Many other mountains described in this book, including Mount Washington, Mount Moosilauke, Mount Greylock, and Mount Mansfield have suffered this dubious honor. The summit hotels have since been destroyed or removed from these mountains, although Mount Greylock still has an AMC lodge on the summit.

Forgiving skiers can at least make the most of this opportunity. The roads often make good ski routes, and the ones on Wachusett are no exception. The park does not allow snowmobiling on the unplowed park roads, although telltale tread tracks can often be found. Skiing up Administration Road to Summit Road offers some of the mountain's nicest vistas. The rivers and lakes that dot southern Massachusetts are the most distinctive land features that can be seen. The descent down the road is an enjoyable beginner telemark run. If descending Summit Road in the opposite direction (turning left as you leave the summit spur road) to the visitor center, watch out for skiers where the unplowed road crosses the two main downhill ski trails. The Wachusett Mountain ski area is not renowned for attracting the most controlled skiers.

Rangers at the visitor center say the rocky hiking trails are not very suitable for skiing. There is some truth to this if the snow cover is thin. However, Wachusett is a worthwhile destination for ski touring if there has been a recent storm, and the unplowed mountain roads are usually a reliable alternative for good skiing even when there is only a light snow cover.

Other Options. Nearby Leominster State Forest offers miles of easy skiing on its network of hiking trails and woods roads. Rangers at the Wachusett visitor center can also offer suggestions regarding other nearby parks and forests that provide good cross-country skiing.

Connecticut

Pine Mountain

THE TOUR A ski tour along the Tunxis Trail over Pine Mountain in northern Connecticut

LENGTH Ski touring center to Indian Council Caves: 3.5 miles; to CT 219: 5.9 miles

ELEVATION Starting: 1,100 feet; high point: 1,391 feet

MAP USGS New Hartford, Connecticut (7.5-minute series, 1984)

DIFFICULTY Moderate

FEE The Tunxis Trail is accessed via trails at the Pine Mountain Ski Touring Center, where a trail ticket must be purchased.

HOW TO GET THERE The Pine Mountain Ski Touring Center is 2 miles south of East Hartland at the junction of CT 179 and Art Hayes Road.

The northern part of Connecticut is home to the largest mountains in the state. The hilly Housatonic River valley is surrounded by the southern end of the Berkshire mountain chain, capped by Mount Frissell (elevation 2,380 feet), the highest mountain in Connecticut, in the northwest corner. Skiers have tended to stay in the valleys rather than ski on these mountains because the trails on them, most notably the

Skiing the Tunxis Trail near Pine Mountain.

Appalachian Trail, are generally too rocky and narrow to accommodate good skiing.

But there is good mountain skiing in Connecticut, if you know where to look. Halfway between the Housatonic and Connecticut rivers lies the town of East Hartland. The town is on a small plateau at 1,200 feet and receives considerably more snow and holds it longer than most other areas in the state. What may be rain in West Granby is often snow in East Hartland, although they are only 4 miles apart by road. There is usually a good snowpack from New Year's Day through mid-March. Also, the soil tends to be more sandy than rocky on this plateau, which means less snow cover is needed to make the trails skiable.

The ski tour on the Tunxis Trail over Pine Mountain (elevation 1,391 feet) is rugged and scenic and is not traveled as frequently as other trails in the area. It mixes a mountain summit tour with a classic southern New England woods route, covering rolling terrain and crossing old farm boundaries as it moves through a pretty softwood forest. The route follows the Tunxis Trail for most of its length. The Tunxis Trail is 42 miles long, running from the Massachusetts border just north of East Hartland to the town of Wolcott in central Connecticut. It is marked by blue blazes for its entire length and is known to many people simply as the "Blue Trail."

The ski tour begins at the Pine Mountain Ski Touring Center, where there is parking. Skiers are warned against parking on CT 179 since police have occasionally ticketed and towed cars that were parked there illegally. Follow the groomed ski touring center trail due west to where it picks up the Pine Mountain Road. This unplowed road within the Tunxis State Forest is groomed for most of its length and forms a horseshoe around the mountain. Turn left on Pine Mountain Road and follow it a short distance until it intersects with the Tunxis Trail (blazed blue) on the left. The wide trail to the summit of Pine Mountain climbs gradually to the south (left), reaching the summit in 0.4 mile. There are views to the east over the Connecticut River valley from the summit ledge. On a clear day, it is possible to see all the way north to Mount Monad-

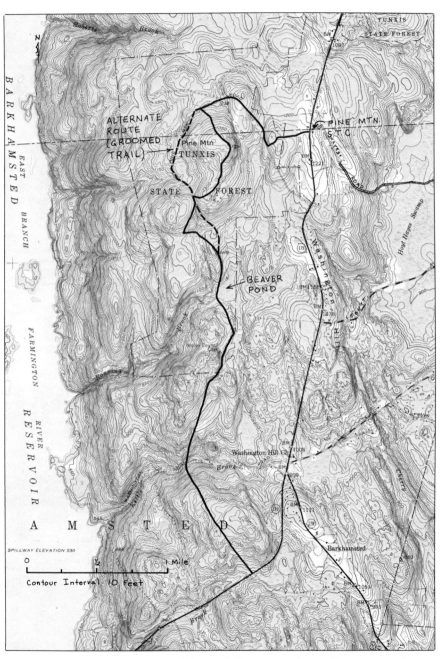

Pine Mountain, Connecticut

nock in southern New Hampshire and southeast to the tower atop Talcott Mountain.

The trail from the summit going south is a narrower hiking path. It descends a rolling ridge, climbing and dipping over small knolls. The final 0.1 mile drops steeply to where it intersects the Pine Mountain Road. The Tunxis Trail continues on the west side of the road. The trail climbs steeply for a short way until a junction is reached. The right-hand junction drops steeply down to the Barkhamsted Reservoir (skiers and hikers prohibited), and the left fork drops moderately to where the Pine Mountain Road ends. The Tunxis Trail continues south from here, passing an old beaver pond with a nice rock on which to take a lunch break. The Pine Mountain Road is groomed and patrolled only to this pond.

The trail continues south 0.4 mile to the Indian Council Caves. The "caves" are actually an interesting collection of house-sized boulders that form cavelike passageways in the spaces between them. They are so named because they were once a landmark where local Tunxis Indian leaders would hold their council meetings.

Skiers may opt to end their tour here. The return via the groomed Pine Mountain Road is an enjoyable trip, with fun downhill sections. It makes for a 7-mile loop tour back to the touring center. For those wishing to continue their southward progress, the Tunxis Trail can be followed another 2.4 miles to where it intersects CT 219. From the Indian Council Caves, the trail drops 350 feet over the next 1.6 miles past the Kettle Brook drainage before climbing gradually back to the road. The trail is well blazed, but a map and compass should be carried. This section of the trail is not skied frequently, so calculate additional time into your trip for breaking trail.

The section of the Tunxis Trail south of the Indian Council Caves is on Metropolitan District Commission (MDC) land. Before heading out inquire at the touring center about the current regulations regarding crossing MDC land, in order to avoid problems. The trailhead on CT 219 is 5 miles south of the touring center, so it will be necessary either to have a car there or to get a ride back. The Pine Mountain Touring Center asks that skiers on the Tunxis Trail sign in and out, so that its staff does not go searching for skiers who have left cars in the parking lot after the center has closed.

Throughout the tour there are often signs of wildlife. Deer can often be seen in the woods, and signs of fox crisscross the area. A rather unusual distinction of this area is that it is home to a large number of wild turkeys. They are responsible for the large bird tracks you may encounter. The turkeys make a sound like a large gust of wind coming at you when they run, and they are surprisingly fast runners.

Rhode Island

Arcadia Management Area

THE TOURS Ski tours in the Arcadia Management Area in southwestern Rhode Island. The Tripp Trail loop goes along the east side of Breakheart Pond and returns on the Bliven Trail. Another ski tour goes over Mount Tom to Stepstone Falls. Many other tours are possible in the park.

LENGTH Tripp Trail loop: 4 miles; Mount Tom Trail to Stepstone Falls: 4.3 miles

ELEVATION Tripp Trail: starting, 200 feet; high point, 450 feet; Mount Tom Trail: starting, 200 feet; high point, 430 feet

MAPS USGS Hope Valley, Rhode Island (7.5-minute series, 1970); AMC Rhode Island Inter-Park Trails map, southwestern section (shows trails but not topography)

DIFFICULTY Moderate

HOW TO GET THERE From I-95, take exit 5-A at the RI 102 interchange and go 0.5 mile east to RI 3. Go south on RI 3 for 1.3 miles; RI 165 leaves to the right, and the Tripp Trail trailhead is 1.5 miles west. You may park at the church, 0.2 mile west of the trailhead. The trailhead for the Mount Tom Trail is at a snowmobile parking lot, 0.9 mile west of the church.

Emerging from the woods on the Bliven Trail in Arcadia Management Area.

If woods skiing through rolling hills and lowland ponds is the way you most enjoy spending a winter day, Rhode Island offers the perfect setting. The western side of this coastal state has large areas of rural countryside dotted by small, rounded hills. The smallest state in the union is small in other ways, too: its highest mountain, Jerimoth Hill, is only 812 feet high.

Arcadia Management Area is the name given to 14,000 acres of park and recreation land clustered just north of the town of Hope Valley. The area used to be divided into several units, including two state parks, but those have now been merged into one jurisdiction. This is an undeveloped region that was once home to a number of farms. Numerous old woods roads that accessed the farms still remain. Some of these are abandoned town roads, and many of them were originally built by the CCC. It is these old dirt and gravel roads that make the area so well suited for ski touring. Since Rhode Island does not get an abundance of snow in the winter, the most reliable terrain for skiing is often these abandoned paths. With their even grade and lack of rocks, they do not require the quantity of snow that rocky hiking trails need in order to be skiable.

There are many ski tours one can take in Arcadia. A good source for ideas is the *AMC Massachusetts and Rhode Island Trail Guide*. The tours described here were chosen for the variety of terrain they cover in the park. They access a woodland pond, a small mountain, and a picturesque waterfall.

The Tripp Trail links several abandoned roads and some foot trails just east of Breakheart Pond. It provides exceptionally pretty woods skiing on wide, easy, graded paths. The trail begins at a metal gate 0.1 mile east of the West Exeter Baptist Church. The Tripp Trail is not shown on any of the available maps, except the one included in this book. There is a sign marking the start of the trail, and occasional white blazes with the image of a skier on them to mark the route. The trail wanders through groves of red and white pine trees, indications of the sandy soil in the area. A number of other trails and abandoned roads dart off from the Tripp Trail, but hold steady to the main path.

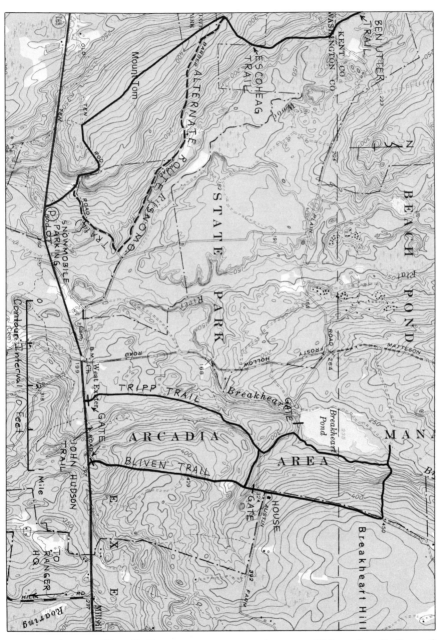

Arcadia Management Area, Rhode Island

After 1.2 miles, be alert for a narrow trail leaving to the right. This is a cutoff trail that leads to the Bliven Trail, also known as the abandoned section of the Austin Farm Road. The cutoff is marked with white skier blazes. A 2.3-mile version of this loop tour can be made if this cutoff is taken. To continue on to Breakheart Pond, follow the Tripp Trail to a major trail junction just beyond the cutoff trail. Turning right here will lead to the Bliven Trail, just north of where the cutoff trail connects. Turning sharply left at the Tripp Trail junction soon leads to the pond, which lies just beyond a metal gate. The ski trail cuts off to the right just before reaching this gate and continues north along the east side of the pond. Breakheart Pond is a popular destination for summer fishermen as well as winter sports enthusiasts.

From Breakheart Pond, the ski trail heads north, contouring alongside Breakheart Hill (elevation 470 feet). At the north end of the pond, the trail turns sharply east and climbs 200 feet over the next 0.3 mile, at which point it makes a right angle turn to the south (right) onto an abandoned section of Breakheart Road. From this junction, it is an enjoyable 1.3-mile downhill ride to the junction with the Bliven Trail, which lies just beyond a large white house. The Bliven Trail climbs a short distance to the top of a small plateau. The skiing up here is delightful, flat, long-stride terrain. The trail then drops from the plateau back to RI 165. The church is 0.6 mile west of the Bliven Trail trailhead.

The ski trail up Mount Tom begins from a snowmobile parking lot on the north side of RI 165, 0.9 mile west of the church. The actual Mount Tom Trail begins 0.5 mile west of here where the road crests a hill, but the original trailhead has been erased by the widening of the road. As a result, the ski trail accesses the mountain from this slightly different route. The ski trail follows abandoned roads to the summit of Mount Tom (elevation 430 feet). From the ledgy summit of the mountain, there is a 360-degree panorama of the surrounding countryside. To the west is the Pachaug State Forest in Connecticut, where there is also good skiing. To the northeast is the forested Breakheart Hill. One can easily imagine the gentle landscape below as the patchwork of farms that it once was. The trail continues over the summit and meets the Barber Road and the Escoheag Trail.

From where the Mount Tom Trail ends at the junction of the Escoheag Trail and Barber Road, the Escoheag Trail can be taken to the Ben Utter Trail to Stepstone Falls. The falls, 2.6 miles from the Mount Tom-Escoheag Trail junction, are a picturesque cascade over a series of ledges.

For the return trip, some variety can be added by skiing back on the Barber Road. This abandoned road is part of the park's snowmobile trail network, but it is also an enjoyable, easy downhill run back to the parking lot. It drops 200 feet in the first 0.7 mile before descending more gradually to a seies of woods road junctions.

Several trails in the park were originally cut by the Narragansett chapter of the Appalachian Mountain Club. Trails such as the Ben Utter and the John Hudson were named for longtime AMC volunteers active in the creation and maintenance of these paths.

The ski season at Arcadia is unpredictable, but it generally falls during January and February. The rule of thumb for skiing in Rhode Island is *don't wait*: ski during and just after the snowfall because it may not last for long. The trails do not require heavy snow cover to be skiable, so be adventurous and plan to ski them even if there has not been a heavy dump. Information on snow conditions may be obtained by calling the Arcadia Management Area headquarters at 401-539-2356.

Other Options. A very popular destination for skiing in Rhode Island is Pulaski State Park in Burrillville. This northwestern corner of the state gets the most reliable snow. The small trail network is groomed and attracts large numbers of people—reasons why I have not selected it as a classic tour. The best times to go to avoid crowds are mid-week and early in the morning on weekends.

Postscript

This book is about the past, present, and—most important—future of skiing. Skiers are picking up where an earlier generation left off and returning to the backcountry on skis. The possibilities of where we can go and what we can explore are limitless.

But the opportunity to travel freely in the backcountry cannot be taken for granted. Old trails are being closed "for our own good," and we are now being told that certain wilderness areas are unsafe to ski.

Take, for example, the case of Cannon Mountain in New Hampshire. It is not included in this book, yet some skiers know that it is home to three of the finest and most historic backcountry ski routes in New England. The Tucker Brook Trail, in particular, is a wonderful run from the summit ridge of Cannon down the northeast side of the mountain. Unfortunately, the Tucker Brook Trail is officially closed to skiers. The U.S. Forest Service and the New Hampshire Division of Parks and Recreation have decided it is unsafe to ski a trail that is unpatrolled, unmaintained, and (they believe) not wide enough. Although the trail may still be skied, it is considered illegal to do so; I have therefore reluctantly omitted the Tucker Brook Trail from this book.

Similarly, in Baxter State Park skiers and mountaineers are strictly regulated by park authorities. They can be denied entry to the park for failing to submit the proper paperwork in time or for lacking "qualifications" to be using the park in winter. The mountain is "closed" by rangers when they determine that weather conditions make travel on the mountain unsafe.

The "freedom of the hills" is a precious experience in this

overregulated, overlitigated world. If we self-sufficient, non-motorized wilderness travelers are to preserve our access to wild places, we must take an active role in fighting some of these misguided bureaucratic regulations. I urge you to join an outdoor organization that works to preserve access to wilderness areas, and to write to your political representatives, making your thoughts known to those officials who can effect change (see appendix A for the names of several outdoor organizations).

Please also consider helping to preserve and restore the ski trails that already exist. Most of the trails in this book are maintained by volunteer labor; it does not take long for a trail to become overgrown and unskiable. If you have a favorite ski trail, inquire locally about who maintains it and offer to pitch in.

Finally, a modest proposal. Surely the talent for building good ski trails did not die with the CCC. Why not initiate new efforts to upgrade some existing ski or hiking trails so that they can be enjoyable ski runs, or even cut a few new ones? This, of course, would have to be approved by the landowners or park authorities who manage the areas. The renaissance of backcountry skiing has potential that is largely untapped. The time is ripe to convert dreams and possibilities into reality.

Appendix A
Outdoor and Instructional Organizations

The following is a selective listing of organizations in New England which offer information or instructional programs related to backcountry skiing. This is by no means a complete list. Most downhill ski areas and ski touring centers now offer telemark lessons in addition to their other classes.

Appalachian Mountain Club
5 Joy Street
Boston, MA 02108

The AMC offers a variety of courses throughout the winter in cross-country downhill skiing, avalanche assessment, ski touring, and mountain safety.

Catamount Trail Association
P.O. Box 897
Burlington, VT 05402

The Catamount Trail is a 289-mile backcountry ski trail that runs the length of Vermont, from the Massachusetts to the Canadian borders. It links more than two dozen ski touring centers along the way. The Catamount Trail Association offers maps and information on the trail, coordinates trail maintenance, and publishes a newsletter. Every February it organizes an "end-to-end relay," a three-week effort to ski the entire length of the trail. Support for the trails comes from member contributions.

Dartmouth College
Office of Outdoor Programs
Box 9
Hanover, NH 03755

The Office of Outdoor Programs of Dartmouth College offers an excellent three-day cross-country downhill workshop every January. It is taught by Adirondack skiers Todd Eastman, Rob Frenette, and their friends, who are as talented as teachers as they are as skiers. Dartmouth also offers other ski clinics and courses in winter mountaineering. These courses are open to the public.

Green Mountain Club
P.O. Box 889
Montpelier, VT 05602

The Green Mountain Club (GMC) is the founder, protector, and maintainer of the Long Trail, the 265-mile-long footpath that runs the length of Vermont. The GMC is divided into fourteen regional sections. Each section organizes its own winter outings, which are open to the public. Contact the GMC at 802-223-3463 for information about the activities of these sections. For a free copy of their informative pamphlet *Winter Trail Use in the Green Mountains*, send a SASE to them at the above address.

Hurricane Island Outward Bound School
P.O. Box 429
Rockland, ME 04841

The Hurricane Island Outward Bound School offers a wide range of winter courses in the White Mountains of New Hampshire and in the Mahoosuc Mountains of Maine. Winter mountaineering, backcountry skiing, and general winter wilderness courses are among their offerings. These courses provide a comprehensive introduction to winter skills.

North American Telemark Organization (NATO)
Box 44
Waitsfield, VT 05673

Dick Hall has been teaching people the basics of cross-country downhill technique for years and has a loyal following of students. He and his fellow NATO instructors offer courses for ski instructors, beginner skiers, and people interested in multiday "adventure ski tours."

Appendix B
Emergency Contacts

New Hampshire

New Hampshire State Police	800-525-5555
Appalachian Mountain Club	603-466-2727

Vermont

Vermont State Police	800-852-3411

Maine

Maine State Police	800-452-4664
Department of Inland Fisheries and Wildlife, Central Coast/Augusta Region (includes Camden Hills and Mount Blue)	800-322-3606
Millinocket Police Department (for Baxter State Park)	207-723-9731

Massachusetts

Massachusetts State Police	800-525-5555

Connecticut

Connecticut State Police   800-842-0200

Rhode Island

Rhode Island State Police   401-647-3311

Note: The toll-free (1-800) telephone numbers can only be used when calling from within the given state.

Glossary

alpine environment   The environment of the high mountains. Exposure to the elements, panoramic views, and challenging traveling conditions are all part of the experience of being in this setting.

alpine skiing   Skiing with equipment designed for downhill travel only, such as on lift-served mountains. The rigid boots and locked heels do not permit climbing.

avalanche   The sudden release of a large quantity of snow down a mountain.

bail   The metal toe-piece on the front of a Nordic 3-pin binding that clamps the toe of a Nordic ski boot onto the pins of the binding.

cable binding   A Nordic binding system that holds the boot in place on the ski by means of a wire cable that wraps around the heel.

camber   The arch in the middle of a ski between the tip and tail.

climbing skins   Ski-length strips of material that glue or strap onto the ski for long climbs. The hairs or scales on the skins prevent backsliding on steep ascents.

committing route   A route that does not allow skiers easy exit.

contouring   Maintaining the same elevation while traveling from point to point.

contour line   A line joining equal elevations on a topographical map.

cross-country skiing   Skiing with lightweight Nordic ski equipment on prepared tracks on gentle terrain.

declination   The deviation between magnetic north (where the compass needle points) and true north (the geographically correct location of the North Pole).

diagonal stride The classic style of cross-country skiing. Skis are moved forward parallel to one another while poles touch the snow alternately.

double boot A two-piece Nordic ski boot composed of an inner boot and an outer shell. Double boots are exceptionally warm.

double poling A modified version of the diagonal stride in which a skier moves forward by pushing off with both poles on alternate strides.

down-mountain skiing The style of downhill skiing in the backcountry popular among New England skiers in the 1930s.

drainage A small valley or ravine formed down a mountainside by moving water.

fall line The straightest line down a slope. It is the path a ball would follow if rolled from the top.

gully A drainage or cleft that often separates rock outcrops.

headwall The steepest upper section of a glacially formed bowl.

herringbone A technique of climbing uphill on skis. The skis are positioned with the tips pointed away from one another as the skier steps up the slope.

Nordic skiing The style of skiing with flexible boots and free heels.

parallel skiing Skiing downhill with skis kept parallel to one another and the uphill ski kept slightly ahead.

schuss To ski downhill without turning.

sidecut The curve cut into the sides of most touring skis. The hourglass shape of the ski makes the ski turn more easily as it follows the arc of the sidecut.

sidehill A trail that traverses across a slope, banking sideways.

skating A technique of skiing that resembles the side-to-side motion of ice skating. A fast, efficient technique for travel on hard-packed snow.

ski mountaineering Traveling in the mountains on skis, which calls upon the full range of mountaineering skills. These include winter camping, snow and ice climbing, and off-trail navigation.

skinning Skiing uphill with climbing skins.

ski touring Skiing both on and off of groomed trails on a variety of terrain, from easy valley tours to challenging mountain routes.

step turn A turn made by stepping in the direction you want to go.

supergaiter A gaiter that covers the entire ski boot from the welt and extends up over the calf. Supergaiters are often insulated to provide additional warmth for the feet.

telemark turn A turn with free-heeled Nordic ski equipment in which the downhill ski is moved forward and the rear knee is bent almost at a right angle.

3-pin equipment The traditional equipment for Nordic skiing: a medium-weight ski, a boot with three small holes punched into the toe, and a binding with three short posts that engage the boot pin-holes. The use of this equipment is the reason why Nordic skiing is sometimes described as "three-pinning," and why avid Nordic skiers are affectionately referred to as "pinheads."

topographic map A map that indicates variations in elevation by the use of contour lines.

traverse To travel across a slope. A traverse is also a high route through the mountains that connects two points, such as the Bolton-Trapp Traverse.

wax pocket The area formed by the camber arch of a ski, halfway between the tip and tail, where wax is placed for optimum contact with the snow.

Annotated Bibliography

What follows is a selection of books that I think do an exceptionally good job in covering their subjects. I have learned a great deal from many of these books. They offer useful pointers on subjects ranging from ski technique to mountaineering. Books and people are great sources of ideas, and information sharing is vital for stimulating new explorations and keeping our sport growing and safe.

Equipment and Technique

Barnett, Steve. *Cross Country Downhill and Other Nordic Mountain Skiing Techniques*. 3d ed. Chester, Conn.: Globe Pequot Press, 1983.

This book was instrumental in the revival of telemarking and other Nordic downhill techniques when it was first published in 1978. It is one of the most informative and helpful guides on ski technique.

Bein, Vic. *Mountain Skiing*. Seattle: The Mountaineers, 1982.

A thorough treatment of all aspects of backcountry skiing and ski mountaineering, from technique to equipment.

Brady, Michael. *Cross-Country Ski Gear*. 2d ed. Seattle: The Mountaineers, 1987.

An extremely detailed explanation of ski equipment. Includes a good discussion on waxing skis.

Gillette, Ned, and John Dostal. *Cross-Country Skiing*. 3d ed. Seattle: The Mountaineers, 1988.

A comprehensive book on skiing, including diagonal skiing, skating, telemarking, parallel, winter camping, and waxing. Gillette is an accomplished skier and mountaineer who enlivens his discussion of skiing with anecdotes from his many adventures.

Tejada-Flores, Lito. *Backcountry Skiing*. San Francisco: Sierra Club Books, 1981.

Tejada-Flores is an excellent writer and an authority on skiing. This books covers all aspects of backcountry skiing, from equipment to technique.

Mountaineering

Cliff, Peter. *Ski Mountaineering*. Chester, Conn.: Globe Pequot Press, 1987.

For skiers interested in the full range of what can be done on skis, this books contains basic discussions of equipment and technique for alpine ski mountaineering and extreme skiing. Includes color photographs and recommended routes.

Daffern, Tony. *Avalanche Safety for Skiers & Climbers*. Seattle: Alpenbooks, 1983.

An excellent, intelligible guide to avalanche assessment specifically written by and for skiers. There are many books on avalanche hazard which do more to confuse interested readers than they do to elucidate. This book is the best I've seen in terms of clarity and practicality, and it includes good photographs.

LaChapelle, Edward R. *The ABC of Avalanche Safety*. 2d ed. Seattle: The Mountaineers, 1985.

A concise guide to the subject for those looking for a quick introduction.

Peters, Ed, ed. *Mountaineering: The Freedom of the Hills*. 4th ed. Seattle: The Mountaineers, 1982.

Though it does not include specific reference to skiing, this book is the most comprehensive reference guide available to all aspects of mountaineering. It contains a wealth of information on everything from navigation to nutrition to winter camping.

First Aid

Lentz, Martha J., Steven C. Macdonald, and Jan D. Carline. *Mountaineering First Aid: A Guide to Accident Response and First Aid Care.* 3d ed. Seattle: The Mountaineers, 1985.

A good, compact field reference guide that is stocked with concise and useful information.

Wilkerson, James A., M.D., ed. *Hypothermia, Frostbite, and Other Cold Injuries.* Seattle: The Mountaineers, 1986.

For those interested in a more in-depth treatment of the physiology of cold injuries. An up-to-date guide to the latest thinking on the ever evolving approaches to treatment.

Wilkerson, James A., M.D., ed. *Medicine for Mountaineering.* 3d ed. Seattle: The Mountaineers, 1985.

The classic text on wilderness medicine. If your interest in first aid goes beyond the Red Cross curriculum (as it should), this book should be a part of your continuing education.

Ski History

Adler, Allen. *New England & Thereabouts—A Ski Tracing.* Barton, Vt.: NETCO Press, 1985.

A well-researched and entertaining history of skiing in New England, the Adirondacks, and the Laurentians. Available from NETCO Press, P.O. Box 106, Barton, VT 05822.

Belcher, C. Francis. *Logging Railroads of the White Mountains.* Boston: Appalachian Mountain Club, 1980.

Fascinating account of this slice of New England history. Skiers venturing to the Pemigewasset Wilderness will be interested to see the maps of where the old railroads went.

Pote, Winston. *Mt. Washington in Winter: Photographs and Recollections, 1923–1940.* Camden, Me.: Down East Books, 1985.

A pictorial and anecdotal history of winter activity in the Presidential Range of the White Mountains, including a great deal of information on skiing. In addition to his breathtaking photographs of skiing in Tuckerman Ravine, Pote's photographs of skiing in some of the less-travelled corners of the Presidential Range should inspire today's skiers to continue exploring.

Waterman, Laura, and Guy Waterman. *Forest and Crag: A History of Hiking, Trail Blazing, and Adventure in the Northeast Mountains.* Boston: Appalachian Mountain Club, 1989.

Brings together the mountain recreation history of the entire northeastern United States. Well written and exhaustively researched.

Guidebooks

Trail Guides—New England

The following trail guides are invaluable sources of information for planning your trips and finding your own "classic" ski tours. All AMC guidebooks come with maps, which are referenced in the route descriptions in this book.

AMC Maine Mountain Guide. 6th ed. Boston: Appalachian Mountain Club, 1988.

AMC Massachusetts and Rhode Island Trail Guide. 6th ed. Boston: Appalachian Mountain Club, 1989.

AMC White Mountain Guide. 24th ed. Boston: Appalachian Mountain Club, 1987.

Appalachian Trail Guides. Harpers Ferry, W.V.: Appalachian Trail Conference.

New England is covered by volumes 1 (Maine), 2 (New Hampshire–Vermont), and 3 (Massachusetts–Connecticut). Trail descriptions are extremely detailed. Available from the AMC or the ATC.

Guide Book of the Long Trail. 23d ed. Montpelier, Vt.: Green Mountain Club, 1987.

Available from the AMC or the GMC.

Ski Guides—New England

Allaben, Stanton. *Vermont Ski Trail Guide*. Londonderry, Vt.: Stanton Allaben Productions, 1983.

This pocket guidebook comes in two volumes: central Vermont and south central Vermont. Route descriptions are not very detailed, but it is a useful resource for finding little-known local trails. Available from Stanton Allaben Productions, 70 Little Pond Rd., Londonderry, VT 05148.

Chamberlain, Lyn, and Tony Chamberlain. *Guide to Cross-Country Skiing in New England*. Chester, Conn.: Globe Pequot Press, 1985.

A good annotated guide to cross-country ski touring centers in New England.

Jackson Ski Touring Foundation. *Ski Trail Guide*. Jackson, N.H.: Jackson Ski Touring Foundation, 1984.

A brief pocket guide to the ski trails in Jackson and Pinkham Notch. Available from the JSTF office in Jackson, or at the Trading Post at the AMC Pinkham Notch Camp.

Perkins, Thom, and Denise Perkins. *New Hampshire Ski Trail Guide*. Londonderry, Vt.: Stanton Allaben Productions, 1983.

A guide to ski tours in the White Mountain region. Capsule descriptions of a variety of trails in the area, including a number of lesser known ones. Available from Stanton Allaben Productions, 70 Little Pond Rd., Londonderry, VT 05148.

Ski Guides for Other Regions

Barnett, Steve. *The Best Ski Touring in America*. San Francisco: Sierra Club Books, 1987.

A catalogue for your dream ski trips. Barnett is well traveled and a good writer. This book makes for good planning or just good reading. The book's one drawback is its lack of good maps.

Burgdorfer, Rainer. *Backcountry Skiing in Washington's Cascades*. Seattle: The Mountaineers, 1986.

Short on prose but long on information. Lists seventy-eight ski routes in one of the most beautiful mountain ranges in the lower United States.

Dawson, Louis W. *Colorado High Routes*. Seattle: The Mountaineers, 1985.

A useful guide to backcountry skiing in the Aspen–Vail–Crested Butte area of Colorado. Describes ninety routes, including the hut-to-hut Tenth Mountain Trail.

Goodwin, Tony. *Northern Adirondack Ski Tours*. Glens Falls, N.Y.: Adirondack Mountain Club Books, 1981.

Don't forget the other great mountain range in the Northeast! The Adirondacks are a match for the White Mountains in the variety and quantity of excellent ski tours they offer. This book lists thirty "selected tours for the novice to expert skier."

Johnson, Randy. *Southern Snow: The Winter Guide to Dixie.* Boston: Appalachian Mountain Club, 1987.

A guide to downhill skiing, cross-country skiing, hiking, and mountaineering in the southern states.

Nature/Ecology

Burk, John, and Marjorie Holland. *Stone Walls and Sugar Maples: An Ecology for Northeasterners.* Boston: Appalachian Mountain Club, 1979.

A synthesis of ecology, natural history, conservation, and outdoor recreation.

Marchand, Peter J. *North Woods: An Inside Look at the Nature of Forests in the Northeast.* Boston: Appalachian Mountain Club, 1987.

An aid to plant identification and a discussion of current ecological research.

Steele, Frederic L. *At Timberline: A Nature Guide to the Mountains of the Northeast.* Boston: Appalachian Mountain Club, 1982.

A field guide to plants, wildlife, and geologic formations.

Maps

Appalachian Mountain Club maps are available from the AMC, 5 Joy St., Boston, MA 02108, and at the Trading Post at the AMC Pinkham Notch Camp, Gorham, NH.

USGS maps can be ordered from the USGS, Box 25286, Federal Center, Denver, CO 80225.

DeLorme Publishing Company, P.O. Box 298, Freeport, ME 04032. Publishes more than fifty maps, atlases, and guidebooks pertaining to northern New England. Its large-scale topographic maps of the White Mountains, Baxter State Park, and Acadia National Park are particularly useful for the routes in this book.

USGS, AMC, and DeLorme maps can also be purchased at a variety of outdoor equipment stores and bookshops throughout New England.

Other sources of maps for New England:

Green Mountain Club, P.O. Box 889, Montpelier, VT 05602.
Publishes annotated topographic maps of Camel's Hump and Mount Mansfield, as well as books and pamphlets about Vermont.

New England Cartographics, P.O. Box 369, Amherst, MA 01004.
Publishes the *Western Massachusetts Trail Map Pack for Backpackers, Hikers, Skiers,* by Christopher J. Ryan, which includes up-to-date topographic maps of Mount Greylock, Wachusett Mountain, and other mountains and parks in Massachusetts.

Northern Cartographic, P.O. Box 133, Burlington, VT 05402.
Publishes the excellent *Stowe Cross-Country Ski Map,* a detailed topographic map edited by Steve Bushey.

Waumbek Books, P.O. Box 573, Ashland, New Hampshire 03217.
Publishes the Washington and Lafayette Trail Maps, two waterproof maps covering the principal ranges of the White Mountains in New Hampshire and Maine.

About the Author

David Goodman is a freelance writer, skier, and mountaineer who has written widely on outdoor and political subjects. His articles have appeared in such publications as *Outside, Cross-Country Skier, Powder,* the *Boston Globe, Boston Magazine,* the *Village Voice, The Nation, Harvard Magazine,* and *Rock & Ice.* He also works throughout the Northeast as an instructor for the Hurricane Island Outward Bound School and is licensed as a wilderness emergency medical technician. In addition to New England, he has skied and climbed in Switzerland, Nepal, British Columbia, and many of the mountain ranges in the western United States. When not out searching for, skiing, or climbing "classics," he lives in Boston.

Photograph by Peter Cole

About the AMC

The Appalachian Mountain Club is a nonprofit volunteer organization of over 35,000 members. Centered in the northeastern United States with headquarters in Boston, its membership is worldwide. The AMC was founded in 1876, making it the oldest organization of its kind in America. It is committed to conserving, developing, and managing dispersed outdoor recreational opportunities for the public and its efforts in the past have endowed it with a significant public trust.

Ten regional chapters from Maine to Pennsylvania, some sixty committees, and hundreds of volunteers supported by a dedicated professional staff join in administering the club's wide-ranging programs. Besides volunteer organized and led expeditions, these include research, backcountry management, trail and shelter construction and maintenance, conservation, and outdoor education. The club operates a unique system of eight alpine huts in the White Mountains; a base camp and public information center at Pinkham Notch, New Hampshire; five full-service camps; four self-service camps; and nine campgrounds, all open to the public. Its Boston headquarters houses not only a public information center but also the largest mountaineering library and research facility in the United States. The club also conducts leadership workshops, mountain search and rescue, and a youth opportunity program for disadvantaged urban young people. The AMC publishes books, maps, and America's oldest mountaineering journal, *Appalachia.*

We invite you to join and share in the benefits of membership. Membership brings a subscription to the monthly bulletin *Appalachia;* discounts on publications and at the huts and camps managed by the club; notices of trips and programs; and association with chapters and their meetings and activities. Most important, membership offers the opportunity to support and share in the major public service efforts of the club.

Membership is open to the general public upon completion of an application form and payment of an initiation fee and annual dues. Information on membership as well as the names and addresses of the secretaries of local chapters may be obtained by writing to: Appalachian Mountain Club, 5 Joy St., Boston, MA 02108, or calling during business hours 617-523-0636.

Stowe's Second Ski Beginning Began Here.

In the woods and fields of the Trapp Family Lodge. First in the 1930s, when the lure of Vermont's woods and hills attracted skiers from around the country. And again in the 60s, when America's current affair with fitness began.

On our groomed tracks, or back country trails and routes.

There's no place quite like the Trapp Family Lodge.

It's a little of Austria, a lot of Vermont.

Trapp Family Lodge
& Touring Center
Stowe, Vermont 05672

1-800-826-7000